T0086190

WHAT DOES THE RESURRECTION OF JESUS CHRIST MEAN TO YOU AND ME?

ARTHUR CHINGWARU

WESTBOW
PRESS®
A DIVISION OF THOMAS NELSON
& ZONDERVAN

WestBow Press books may be ordered through booksellers or by contacting:

WestBow Press
A Division of Thomas Nelson & Zondervan
1663 Liberty Drive
Bloomington, IN 47403
www.westbowpress.com
844-714-3454

All Scripture quotations are taken from The Holy Bible, New International Version®, NIV® Copyright © 1973, 1978, 1984, 2011 by Biblica, Inc.® Used by permission. All rights reserved worldwide.

ISBN: 978-1-9736-9963-7 (sc)
ISBN: 978-1-9736-9965-1 (hc)
ISBN: 978-1-9736-9964-4 (e)

Library of Congress Control Number: 2023909851

Print information available on the last page.

WestBow Press rev. date: 6/12/2023

CONTENTS

In John 11:25 (NIV) Jesus said He was "the resurrection and the life." We will all die, but what comes next will depend on our faith. Not all will see a second death; there will be the resurrection of the souls. It is wise to commit our lives to Him, because He has power over life and death.

The resurrection is the basis for the church's witness to the world: Jesus's bodily resurrection shows us that He is living and that He has authority and power even over death and that He rules over eternity. His blood that flowed on the cross brings a new covenant. Now we can witness to the world that He is alive, which we can say without any hesitation because He spent forty days with us after His resurrection before His ascension.

He is a risen Christ who is living and controls everything and is now intercessor between God and us. We must be happy that He is in intercession for us. We have an assurance that we will rise, and this is coming from the one who Himself defeated death and is alive. Let us follow Him

INTRODUCTION

There could not be any Christianity if there were no resurrection. God planned this long before it happened. What was happening needed a revelation. It would not have been thought of as leading to the resurrection. This was prefigured as far back as Genesis 3:15 where the devil was told that the serpent's head would be crushed.

The love that God had for humanity at creation persisted to the resurrection and carries on to this day.

But the forces of darkness have not given up; they also are still persisting. They are trying to make earthly things as attractive as they can be so that they are enticing to us.

God's plans are still being implemented to this day; He is using people He chooses to use to further His will on earth. The resurrection was done in order for us to get salvation, confirming God's love. That is why at Easter, there is a day called "Good Friday," which means what happened at Calvary that day is good for us.

There are Scriptures that tell us about the crucifixion and the resurrection, because God knows what is good for us. These Scriptures also tell us about obedience to God. As a result of our obedience to Him, He will love us, and He will make us the way He wants us to be. He makes us know that the resurrection is for our salvation. The Scriptures teach us that by following Him, we are following the true path of life.

Following Him who rose from the dead means we will also rise from the dead. What we have seen happening to Him should be proof enough for us to accept Him as true saviour. For us to qualify to be called His children, we must try to stay away from sin and ask Him to lead us not into temptations, because sin defiles us.

We are following a man whose ways prove that He is worthy to be followed. The good thing about Him is that He imparted some of His powers to us. He selected some men that He travelled with for three years. This was to prepare them to take over at His time of leaving the earth. These men also handed over to us when they were also to leave, so there is a continuity of the work. The reason why He wants His work to continue is because He wants all souls to be brought into the fold. He wants our characters to reflect His character so that whoever is asked to come to the fold will have no doubt but will know that there is eternity.

The fact that He rose from the dead will encourage belief in His story. The Christian religion is named after Him. It is not all smooth sailing; there are some who are opposed to Him, just as such differences led Him to be crucified, and they thought that in that way they had gotten rid of Him. But when the third day came, the grave and death became powerless. That event brought into being the new covenant that makes us the sons and daughters of God for everlasting.

The resurrection reminds us to accept Jesus in our hearts, as He is the Son of God. That means we will be the children of God also. We are advised to give ourselves to God, and whatever He says, we obey, and our relationship will last forever.

His love to us is that even if we try to hide from Him, He will still look for us, to let us also return that love. Jesus came specifically to restore our relationship with God; that is part of the good news that He brought and is part of His mission on earth.

We have been given a second chance and a second choice. This time we should not lose it again, because Jesus is on our side. His love to us never ends.

CHAPTER 1

IN THE BEGINNING WAS THE WORD

Without going round and round, the word is truly God, so there is no more having any doubts in our minds. We are to know that we are talking about God who, because of His love to humanity, became flesh and dwelt among us so that He would be exemplary. By doing that, He gave us something to emulate and also leads us to become models before the world. That is His goal: that we take it from where He left off. Let us take this advice with the spirituality it deserves. Now we know for certain that He was at creation, so we are letting people know that when we are talking of the resurrection, this is how it all came about.

The Resurrection all started with the virgin being told that she was a chosen vessel among women and that she would have a child and would call His name Jesus. He would be born in a manger, but before that, there was a word in the beginning. This word was with God; the word was God. When we hear the story of the resurrection, we have to cast our eyes near and far, in order for us to know that He is the creator of all things. So before we think of anything else, we have to bear in mind that Jesus is supreme to everything. In Him everything holds together. We must not distance ourselves from Him, knowing that He loves what He created.

God formulated a plan, which was to make His Son a sacrifice. That meant that He had to come to earth as a human being; that is why all these were involved. When God made this plan of sending Jesus into the earth, He did not just come as an ordinary man. He was both divine and human, so that way Jesus was unique. However, that should not stop us from striving to be like Him, because He said, "be in me and I will be in you, and we will be one" (see John 17:20–23). He also said He is in the Father, which means it will be a family of the heavenly people made holy by the Father.

Jesus is always dependent on God; that is why He is divine. We can also be divine if we are dependent on Him, who is dependent on God. We are not worth anything if we are not dependent on Jesus; that is why He says, He is the way, the truth, and the life (John 14:6); any who surrender themselves to Him will live.

John 1:1 (NIV) Jesus came here on earth to set an example. If we emulate Him, it will mean what we do will be tied to what we say, because that is what Jesus did. What Jesus taught and did are tied inseparably. The lesson we should learn from Him is that He was not corrupted with this world. We should always ask Him to give us those divine powers to be able to also resist corruption, which is the only way we can get eternal life. Without His divine powers we may not be able to resist the temptations of this corrupt world.

Jesus never ceased to be eternal, so He preserved His divinity to the end. The resurrection was the climax of all that was the word which became flesh (see John 1:1, 9–10, 14). All this was God's plan of salvation of humankind to make that word into flesh in order to be a model of our lives. It is for us to emulate and live.

We should not read the Bible like any other book but treat it with the holiness that it deserves. For

Him to be born of flesh was not the beginning, but only a fulfilment of His love. It teaches us that there is something called prehuman. Jesus came to restore our relationship with God, which was broken by the devil.

The resurrection shows the great power of God to every creation. It gives the happiness that Christ is alive and that He is with us all the time. It is very relieving to Christians to realise that wherever you are, He is with you. This brings us to the true fact that He refused to be made king of the Jews, although they insisted that He should be. He would be confined to one geographical area, but now He is with us wherever we are. There is nothing that He said which did not come to pass; there is every reason to believe in Him.

The belief that He died and rose from the dead is the reason why people celebrate Easter. That is why we call it Good Friday, for someone has died in our place. To all Christian believers, it means that life has power over death, but the devil keeps on wanting to implant a fear in people's hearts that death has power. In actual fact, it has no power at all; nor does that deceiver, but he only wants to implant fear and to get as many people on the side of darkness as possible.

CREATION

According to the *Concise Oxford English Dictionary*, "Creation is the act of bringing something into existence." When we are saying Jesus was there at creation, we are saying everything came into existence through Him. When we talk of the world coming into order, creation is the work of God. Jesus is one of the Trinity; therefore Jesus is part of God, since He is part of the Trinity.

Jesus, being the Son of God and also part of the Trinity, was present during creation (see John 1:1–2). There was a word in the beginning, and this word was with God, and the word was God. This means He was in the beginning with God. Under the direction of the Father, Christ formed and organised the earth. He divided light from darkness to make day and night. He formed the sun, moon, and stars.

Jesus is now in heaven at the right hand of God the Father. Biblically, Jesus is in an actual place called heaven, a place of glory where God dwells with His angels and redeemed children. God created the earth and all that is in the earth, but God dwells with us. In another sense, Jesus is also with us here, in this world.

CHAPTER 2

IT ALL STARTED IN A MANGER

This is a unique king because no other king on earth was ever born in a manger. His mission was designed in such a way that it would end on the cross. We are required to ask for a revelation; sometimes we lack a revelation. That is why when you and I have a vision, we will have to give glory to Him who gives the vision.

When we say the resurrection was God's plan of salvation, we need to look at it from another angle. We find that when we say that the resurrection started in a manger, it will make sense to say that even being born in a manger was God's plan. God's plan for the salvation of humankind started long before humans could think of asking for salvation. That is why it is said, we receive salvation not because of our works but by grace alone, because all that was the plan of God; it came before anyone's works by grace alone.

This does not mean that we should disobey God; no, we should obey, but knowing that the grace was there before the obedience. Obedience and grace will work in coordination. When Jesus said, "I will be in you and you in me," He was adopting us to be the children of God. We must not hesitate to call ourselves the children of God, because of this adoption that was done by Jesus.

WE ARE THE CHILDREN OF GOD

When God said, "Let us make mankind in our image" (Genesis 1:26 NIV), God did not mean a physical image but the spirituality of God. This means that humans are to have dominion over every creation, ruling over it. This means we have been given responsibility over every creation. God created the jewel of all the creation. In return, a person must glorify God, because we were honoured beyond what could be explained.

In other words, as God is divine, so we are also divine. Sometimes we are throwing this divinity away, thinking that we are inferior to be called divine, yet we are, created in the image of God. The reason why we fail to claim that we are divine is that we fail to produce all the attributes of God. That is where sometimes we go wrong because we start taking it as a right to do what we want with nature. In doing so, we are abusing the dominion status conferred on us at creation.

The likeness of God means that if God is love, we are also love. We should be happy that we are in the likeness of God—not to boast about it but to be responsible for every creation. We must welcome the responsibility on us that, because we are offspring of God, we have to behave like Him. Given that responsibility, we have to be very careful because we will be held answerable for that responsibility. He will want to take stock of our lives on the judgement day.

It all started when God said, "Let us make mankind in our own image." That means already He loves someone He made in His own image. We must not be complacent about that love; rather, we should ensure that we give glory to the Lord for such love. God did not end there, when He had created humankind in His own image, the devil came and tried to break the relationship that was there between God and His beloved creation. The devil deceived them into sinning against God. Then the relationship between God and humanity was broken. Now we fail to achieve the attributes of God, which are humanity, goodness, love, and mercy. Humanity was to be condemned to death for ever, but because of his love, we were saved.

SIN CAUSES NAKEDNESS IN THE EYES OF GOD

The devil was happy to see humanity in a state of guilt. Because of that first disobedience to God, we are still continuing to disobey God, but each time we disobey, we appear naked in the eyes of God. By feeling that we are naked we are trying to distance ourselves from God because we are ashamed to face Him.

God had another plan to restore that relationship. This time the plan was to send His only Son into the world to die for our sins, which He did at Calvary, where He ransomed and redeemed us for ever. Now humanity has to give glory to Him for such love, which came before we asked for it. Such prevenient grace we should never forget but give glory for ever.

Our joy is the result of the suffering that He went through on the cross at Calvary (Ephesians 1:6–10). We have to rejoice that through Jesus Christ, we are able to be called the children of God and to inherit all the heavenly riches.

The precious plan of the salvation of man started on the throne of God; that is when He made a plan to send His Son to be a sacrifice of the sins of man. In trying to clarify what the resurrections means to humankind, it may be prudent to let the reader know that the resurrection was God's plan of salvation for us, but it did not all start at the resurrection. It all started when all the guest rooms were fully booked. That sometimes makes God's plan appear complicated when it is not yet revealed to us, yet even finding no place for the baby to be born was part of God's plan of salvation. We are to receive this salvation by accepting that this was done to save us from the oppression of the devil.

We need a help from Him to get a better understanding of His plan of salvation, since it happened that all the rooms were occupied such that there was not even a single room for the saviour to be born. Are we not having the same situation when we fail to accommodate Jesus in our hearts?

OUR HEARTS ARE PREOCCUPIED WITH EARTHLY THINGS

Nakedness might mean both physical and spiritual when we are disobeying God. We are being naked in front of Him because He expects us to be perfect in our deeds in order to appear to be dressed in front of Him. We have to be careful in our deeds. especially in marriages. We have to be faithful and do only what is required in our lives. We should fear sin, no matter how small we may think it is. Who are we to classify these sins? We do not know how He will judge us. If on the judgement day we are condemned, it means death— and this is the second death which is a spiritual death. After dying a physical death, that will mean failing to qualify for eternal life.

The problem is, are our hearts so preoccupied with earthly things that there may be no room for the saviour in our hearts? It would be prudent to remind the reader of the importance of Jesus coming to earth to save us from the bondage of Satan. This must give us a desire to have Christ born in our hearts instead of Him being accommodated by animals, when in reality, He has come for our souls (Luke 2:7). Jesus is being born as an ordinary person; nothing suggests this could be the Messiah. Even to this day Christianity is still regarded as a second-class matter; we are preoccupied with earthly things that appear to be very attractive in our eyes.

What happened in a manger that day had been long prophesied in the Old Testament—in Deuteronomy, in Isaiah, and in some of the Psalms. God's plan was to make Jesus come to earth in human form, which He did by being born in a manger, by the virgin Mary. The Lord has done His part to show us that He loves us and has shown His plans to save us. It is now up to us to receive this salvation by having faith.

CHAPTER 3

JESUS CHRIST IS ETERNITY

Eternal life is something of its own kind. Just as saying, "Jesus was crucified, died, and was resurrected," it is something unique which was done to save us from the chains of the devil. This was done in order to give us eternal life. That is why we say Jesus is eternity, and He decided to share that eternity with us. We must be able to receive such extended love. In sharing that eternity with us, we could say Jesus has extended a hand, and we in response must extend our hands to receive it.

In simple and straightforward language, eternal life is meant for us, but we must be ready to show that it is meant for us. When we do that, we become one with Christ, because He wants us to be like Him. Whatever

He did was for us to emulate. Eternity means life continuing after death, and we know very well that Jesus died and rose from the dead, so He is eternity

GOD IS STILL USING PEOPLE TODAY

The Lord chooses anybody He will to further His work, as He did to Phillip to go and meet the Ethiopian eunuch (Acts 8:26), because the Lord wanted His word to spread. We have to recognise that even today there are some times when we might not recognise that the Lord wants His word to spread all over the world. This He does by sending us to do it.

Does the way we talk to other people make them want to come to Christ? The way we walk, whatever we touch with our hands, and the way we conduct ourselves must make others want to come to Christ. When Jesus said, "Go and make disciples" (Matthew 28:19), He was saying all our deeds must be preaching. The goal is that everyone will see our good works and want to be like Christ.

What happened long ago that they could not recognise the Messiah when He was among them may still be happening to this day. Sometimes we miss the call because we want signs and events to show us that they are from God. This is not going to happen, but meanwhile we keep on going against His will. Although we are not pastors or preachers, we must be people who fear God, meaning that we must be willing to do good to everyone.

When you asked to do anything, no matter how humble, you must do it to the best of your ability, knowing that you are working for the Lord. When the Lord is using us, we must ask to be guided because without His guidance we are nothing. We are always dependent on Him, so we must know that we have a relationship with God, a relationship of Father and child, and we must maintain that. In other words, what the Father does, the Son must do, so if we are to bring people to Him, we must do exactly as He does so we are like Him.

We must bear in mind that we emulating the divinity that is in Him, which means we must act divinely. It is not difficult to do; it is simply emptying yourself to Him so that He can use you according to how He wants you to be. The Trinity's relationship is so close that they work intimately together as the Father, the Son, and the Holy Spirit. Whenever God chooses one of us to do His work (Acts 9:15), we must not question Him or to go against His will. We cannot direct Him to do His work, as He chooses who He wants. He chose Saul, who later became Paul, because He wanted him to go to the Gentiles.

Even today, God still wants His work done; let us all say, "I am here, Lord," and He can use us. When some tasks are becoming difficult, we start saying God is not involved, but hear what God is saying: "He must suffer for my name's sake." Sometimes God makes us suffer; it is not that He is not there or that He does not know about it, but we must suffer for His name. Sometimes we underrate that God has chosen us to be His vessels. He is delighted to see His gospel flourish because of us. He wants to use us for the furtherance of His word.

God is still speaking to people today. We might expect God to be speaking to us in the same way as He did in the olden days, but it would not be the same because we are in the new covenant. So we must be able to adapt to the new covenant and hear God speak to us.

Jesus promised us before His ascension that He would send us the Comforter, who would be with us. This is the Holy Spirit who has dwelt among us; He is talking to us every day, guiding us in the path of God and telling us to do the things of God. We must bear in mind only that, even though we are living in the world of technology, hardships will always be with us because He Himself went through such hardships as well. We must not despair when these things happen to us, because He might need to test how strong we are in our faith. Nothing we meet on this earth should separate us from His love, because all His suffering was for us to get salvation in the end.

When they say God flourishes in the hearts of the people, God has to be seen in the world through the hearts of the people. It is true to say that God should first work in our hearts and transform them. It is not that simple, as when we say that God should manifest from our hearts, there are many forces that are working against the light that they will keep on trying but the light will always prevail. In John 1:5–9, it says the darkness tried but failed because the darkness failed to overcome the light; it still fails today, even though it keeps on trying.

As is said, God only looks at the heart of people if He wants to use us. God is waiting to use us in His vineyard, which is the world, but God is still doing as He did to young David when He wanted to choose him as king.

There were his brothers, who looked able-bodied, but his choice did not descend on them. God is still doing that to this day, let us stay on our guard knowing that God is still at work as before. Let us submit ourselves to Him, knowing that our lives are in His hands.

He is the light of the world; we can also be the light of the world if we are in Him. To avoid walking in the darkness, we must surrender our lives to Him who is the light, so that we can also be the light like Him. So the best is to ask Him to transform our hearts so that whenever He wants to use us, He will find our hearts fit to be His vessels, which He can use anytime He wants to.

REFLECTION ON OUR LIVES

In our lives we have failures and successes, but it seems we dwell on what we did wrong, and that holds back our progress in life. We must try to encourage ourselves to concentrate on whatever is positive so that it will encourage us to make progress in life rather than being held to ransom by the wrongs we did. Yet if we concentrate on what we did right and seek to improve on that, we can make good progress in our lives and find them full of positives. Our lives have to be built on those lines.

Sometime it is good to write a record of your deeds so that they are not easily forgotten. After you have identified your strengths and positives, take time to read what you have written before; that may help you to recall what you did well. Reflection is very important in our lives, for that will empower us to want to do more or to do better. When you do write such a record, it will help you to recall what might have been forgotten if it was only verbal. This helps to better your life because you will be improving in many ways in your life.

With what God did for us and what He is still doing, we should glorify His name. We can always glorify God if we have faith in Him. To always have faith pleases Him. We know of the things that please God, but sometimes, knowingly we may want to please our flesh (see John 17:3). What is required is to reflect on where we went wrong in our lives. We must confess in order to enable us to move on; that is, He is faithful enough to accept us into the relationship that leads to eternal life. He has truly loved us by sending His Son into the world that anyone who believes in Him should not perish but have everlasting life.

We should always strive to accept God in our lives. By doing so, we are working for eternity. We must be able to put away the things of this world and do only the things that please God. Love the Lord with all your mind and all your strength, and do not forget to fulfil all the requirements such as loving your neighbour as yourself.

This does not mean that when you are saved, you can go on to commit new sins and expect to keep your salvation. Jesus made us to know when He said, "Neither do I condemn you. I will also let you go, but sin no more" (see John 8:11). When you confess your sins and you are saved, stay pure from sin so that you keep your salvation. When saved, always ask to be guided by the Holy Spirit so that you sin no more.

Eternal life means entering into personal relationship with Jesus, meaning that when you have relationship with Jesus, you have also relationship with God because He is in God. Because they are eternity, you will also have eternal life. When we say that God and the Son will exist forever, we mean that when you believe in them, you will also exist forever. His eternal nature is everlasting, meaning that He will exist for ever.

JESUS EXISTED BEFORE 4 BC

It is a fact of life that Jesus existed before the time that He was said to have been born in 4 BC. He already existed, which means He is eternity. In the Trinitarian interpretation, Christ is identified with pre-existent divine hypostasis (substantive reality) called *logos*, meaning word. There is an aspect of divinity in that pre-existence. In John 1:15, 18, John the Baptist testified, "He existed before me." Jesus is divine.

Jesus has two distinct natures. Jesus had all the divine power that He was supposed to have as a divine person. He is both God and man; whoever has seen Jesus has seen God. This was God's plan of salvation to humanity: to dwell among us so that He would show us the way we should live—a life of righteousness. Although we are living in a corrupt world, we must come out clean the way He did.

Jesus did not perform His miracles just make people see His powers, but for a purpose. For instance, when He brought Lazarus to life after he had been in the grave for four days, even Lazarus' sisters were not happy because they said why was Jesus to do such a thing because they said he was already smelling. Sometimes we want to tell God what to do. Jesus wanted to show people that there was life after death and to show us that we will rise again if we have faith in Him (see Colossians 1:17).

He cares for us; that is the reason why He wants us to stay as pure as He is. He also teaches us to look after ourselves so that we become like Him. He is the Prince of Peace because He restores all broken relationship. He sustains everything that is created. By believing in Him we can be guaranteed eternal life. Jesus is good to us because whatever He has, He wants to impart it to us. Because He is eternity, He wants us to have eternal life, because that is His purpose in coming to earth. He is alpha and omega, the first and the Last, so to put our faith in Him means putting our faith in the one who has everything.

CHAPTER 4

GOD'S LOVE FOR HUMANKIND

It becomes a network when it is said God so loved us that He gave His only begotten Son. Now, we would like to return the love by also loving Him with all our strength and with all our minds.

It is up to us to respond to such loving kindness as extended to us by the Lord. If we accept it, that means we have accepted Him in our hearts, and the love that He has to us has got to be reciprocal so that there may be a good relationship between God and His children. God loved the whole world, but when He gave His Son, how much we have accepted Him in our hearts is what makes the difference.

When Jesus was on earth, He showed us the way we

should live because He Himself sympathised with the poor, the widows and the orphans. For us to be able to do as He did, we have to ask the Holy Spirit to guide us and strengthen us so that we can emulate His mission on earth. He even said it was His commandment that we love one another (John 15:12). Jesus is saying the heart must show love first; then however you act towards your neighbour will be good because love is coming from the heart.

We cannot say we love God when we do not love our neighbour. Yet we say we are emulating Jesus Christ, who said He is the true vine saying that if all the branches are intact to the vine, they will bear fruit. This means that if we are attached to the vine, we will bear the same fruit. The best we can do is to invite Christ to stay in our hearts because Christ Himself is love; by inviting Him, we are inviting love into us (John 13:34–35). God has equal love to us, but the difference arises in how we respond to that love, because we all respond in different ways. That will make the difference.

God is our shepherd who, when He loses one sheep, goes on looking for the lost sheep and rejoices when He finds it. God did the same for us. Ehen the devil had decided to snatch us from Him, He sent His Son into the world to redeem us. No matter what sins you have committed before, confess wholeheartedly, and you will be forgiven. Paul murdered many Christians but was forgiven and made an apostle of the Lord.

GOD LOVES THE WORLD

Love is patient, love does not envy, is not self-seeking, and keeps no record of wrongs; love is not easily angered, is not proud, and is not boastful (see 1 Corinthians 13:4–5). God's love for us came before we even knew or asked for it (John 3:16). He already loved us, so it means we had done nothing to deserve that love. That is why we should return that love by doing everything we can to show our obedience and appreciating such love.

To consolidate that love, He makes everything possible to us. Whenever God says anything to us, it may appear impossible, but He never asks us to do anything that He did not do Himself. When He says, "Love Me," He Himself demonstrated it by loving us in such a way that He gave His only Son. Let us love Him; let us love one another as He loved us. God help us to take this demonstration seriously, for if we have such love, surely heaven is awaiting us. If we would demonstrate such love, surely the heavenly kingdom will have come on earth.

We are being called to prepare for eternal life. To us it may appear very remote, but we are being promised. Let us have trust and confidence in Him who loved us before we loved Him. He will not forsake us or let us down. He sent His only begotten Son, and to show our gratitude at receiving such love, we have to give all the glory to Him. It is not giving glory out of nothing but as a way of responding to that love. The reason why God loved humankind before they loved Him is that He is our Father. The father loves His children. We know that we are sinning against Him every day, but He forgives us and gives us another chance. All that He did in giving us His only Son, He did before we even asked for it, but we must return such love by being faithful to Him.

CHAPTER 5

JESUS LIVED WHAT HE PREACHED

Jesus suffered and died on the cross for our sins. By doing that, He was showing us that we cannot say we love our neighbours without sacrificing for them. He sacrificed His life for our sins; by doing that He was showing us that we can also do it for others.

We cannot do it on our own without asking for help from Him to give us the divine strength to be able to overcome the forces that try to pull us down and make us fail to accomplish what we aim to do. Jesus cared for the poor; we must also love and care for the poor and learn to sacrifice what we have for others who might be less fortunate than us. Since Jesus has left the earth, He expects us to continue His work because He commissioned us to continue His work on earth. He loved the little children; we must also love the little children. The church must be in one accord to be able to continue His mission on earth, which He entrusted to the church. If the church does that, they are doing it for the glory of the Lord, whose name will be glorified.

SCRIPTURE IS A LIGHT TO A PERSON'S PATH

Psalm 119:105 makes this point. Sometimes we forget and want to lead ourselves, and we end up walking in darkness because no one is guiding us. In our lives, we must always be asking for divine guidance. When we have done that, we will have a lamp guiding our feet. That means wherever we may go, our way is lit by the Holy Spirit. If we walk by consultation, we will always be guided in the right path which leads to righteousness in life.

We must not try to walk on our own without any guidance from Him who declared that He is the light of the world. In our lives we always want to distinguish between right and wrong. We cannot do that on our own but must ask to be led and guided by Him in our lives. This tells us that the Scriptures will open our minds in such a way that we are no more walking in darkness where we stay without knowing who we are or what to do or not knowing that someone created us

What will enable us to accomplish all that is reading the Scriptures, for everything we need for guidance is in His Word. The Scriptures were inspired in order to guide us through the righteous ways. Always the Scriptures have got answers for what we need in our day-to-day lives.

When we pray for guidance, we must do it in truth and in spirit because that is what is required of us to do. As Christians we must strive to keep the value of Christianity, which will keep Christianity from losing its holiness. Jesus's mission was to redeem the people though living a perfect life. We must also try to live a perfect and blameless life as a follower of Jesus. If people see our good life and follow, we have preached to them through our deeds. That means we have lived a life as we have preached it. All that Jesus did from birth through His life until death and His resurrection was to follow in order for us to have eternal life.

OBEDIENCE IS WORTH SACRIFICE

First Samuel 15:22 (NIV) says, "To obey is better than sacrifice." This simply means that before you need to make a sacrifice, you will have done the right thing that pleases God, and there is no need to make a sacrifice to please God. This is good because once you have done the obedience, already God is pleased with you. You will always be walking beside Him, and the Lord will always be pleased to say whatever He wants to say, knowing that you will always do as He wishes you to do.

This still affects us today, because you do not have to sin purposely, just because you know that when you confess, you will be pardoned. Should we keep on sinning just because God is merciful? No; we have to be obedient in the first place; let us stay clean. Whatever God tells you to do, it has to be exactly as it is said by Him, not as you want it to be.

That means we will not need to offer any sacrifice, because to offer sacrifice is to say, *I have disobeyed; therefore cleanse me.* Obedience applies even when we are dealing with other people; it means whatever agreements you make with other people, you are able to keep them.

Other people will put their trust in you, knowing that you do not break your promise. If you are obedient, you are able to humble yourself. You are sincere in your dealings with others; you can show others that you are devoted in whatever you do.

To be obedient is blessed because you are able to obey even your own rules, and even those who are subordinate to you can still obey them. Also, in our lives, we must recognise that the Holy Spirit will help us obey what is required of us to do. Obedience is wonderful because it helps us to succeed in our lives. Obedience helps us to unlock blessings in our lives and helps us succeed in life. This cannot always happen automatically without asking for guidance from the Holy Spirit, who comes to us through prayers.

Jesus taught love. He showed it by giving love Himself and taught us to be obedient. He was Himself obedient to the will of the Father until the will of the Father was done on the cross. This teaches us to live a life that we preach and not to live a life that is opposite to what we teach. The early church looked after widows and orphans. That should not be for the past only but should always apply to the present day. Jesus in showing us the way He went through life in its fullness, He never took any shortcuts but lived life as it should apply to us, and taught His disciples to do the same.

GIVE YOURSELF TO JESUS, AND HE WILL MOULD YOU

Jeremiah 18:1–6 teaches that it is very unwise of us to think that we can do these things on our own, without His assistance. We are like clay which without a porter will stay clay, not shaped into anything useful. That is why it is always good to put ourselves in the hands of the Lord who will mould us according to the way He desires for us. Then we are in good shape if we are according to His requirements and wishes. We will be better off if we are moulded as He wishes us to be.

In the Old Testament we have examples of people who obeyed prophecies and were saved. For example, the people of Nineveh obeyed the message that was brought by Jonah the prophet, and they were saved from the wrath of God and from destruction. Always trust in the Lord, and He will mould you the way He prefers and the way He wishes. He always wants us to be like Him. By giving ourselves to Him, we will have done exactly as He wishes.

He wants all of us to be in good shape, but sometimes, we take the wrong direction, where the Lord does not wish us to be. "I want you all for Myself," He says, because that is His wish for us. The truth is that if God moulds our hearts as His, we will be all right because He has a good heart, which we always long for all the time of our lives. That means our lives will be full of holiness like Him. If we humbly ask Him to, by His grace He can transform us into His own children He loves. The desires of our hearts are what matters most because we should always desire to be good

The good thing with Jesus is that if you give yourself to Him, He will mould you and make you the way He knows is good. When the disciples travelled with and stayed close to Him for three years, in the end even their accent was like that of Jesus. That means even their behaviour was like that of Jesus, but what I would ask for is to be given a heart like that of Jesus. Then there is no point in asking for His kingdom to come because His kingdom will manifest in me. Hence people will see the heavenly kingdom in me.

CHAPTER 6

JESUS IS THE WAY, THE TRUTH, AND THE LIFE

Jesus did not mince these words in John 14:6 (NIV), but it seems they fall on deaf ears, because there are some who can still doubt that and think that they will find their own way to the Father. Jesus's mission on earth was to let people know and learn from the real person, not to hear it from someone else. He came to demonstrate that He was really the way, the truth, and the life. Jesus said these words during His farewell discourse, but even His disciples did not understand Him until it happened.

The Truth is something verified and found to add up to the standard of what is required of it. Would anyone want to go astray? If so, it will be their own choice. According to Jesus, we should strive to know Him, then knowing the Father will be automatic. Jesus told His apostles that His purpose in coming to earth was to reveal the Father. The good thing with Jesus was that whatever He had, He transferred it to His disciples. Like when He said all power was given to Him from heaven, he immediately transferred that power to the disciples, which means that power has been transferred to us, because the apostles did not take that power with them but left it with us.

Jesus did not say, I want to show you the way to the Father, but He said He is the way. He is not telling the truth, but He *is* the truth. He is not promising us life but as He Himself rose from the dead, He is alive. Following Him means your way is leading you to eternal life. This is what we are all working for—to live for ever, so Jesus comforted His disciples with those words.

They were told from prophecy that there would come the Messiah, but it appeared too remote until the Messiah came. It appears we are also not taking any heed of it, just as they did. When the Messiah came, people thought He was one of the prophets. When it is preached that there will be a second coming, we seem not to take it seriously. But definitely, the second coming is imminent, and we are not taking any heed of it. We ask the Lord to give us a revelation so that it is opened to us of this second coming before we perish. When Jesus preached, He preached of the reality without fear or favour. Jesus, when He preached, He used to remind us to always look after the widows and the orphans, because His eye is on them.

GOD REVEALS HIMSELF IN DIFFERENT WAYS

Jesus put all the emphasis on the fact that no one will go to the Father but through Him. This demonstrates that He is the only one we can call the way, and there is every truth in Him, and in the end, we will not die because He is life.

According to how things are, there is no way we should try to avoid Him. He did everything to show us that He and the Father were one, so there is no way we love the one and hate the other; why try to separate them? If we want to know the truth, Jesus is the source of the truth. The truth is presentation of things as they are and not trying to put them in your own way. Mathematically things will add up well if Jesus says He and His Father are one. He goes on to ask us to be in Him, and He will be in us, that means to say that we will be interwoven in the Trinity. There is some sort of inferiority complex because we think that to claim that we are in the Trinity could be a sin, but that is a fact of life. Jesus is then a reality of all God's promises. He joins His life to ours so that we can also be fit for heaven. We should be modelling our lives to His life. If we do, there is no way we will go wrong. We only go wrong when we try to make our own way of living that is not according to what He said it should be.

JESUS CAME TO SHOW US THE WAY

When Jesus was teaching His disciples that the wider way leads to destruction (Matthew 7:13), He meant that things that seem to make our flesh happy may make us forget that we must work for the Lord. Working for the Lord is doing good. When Jesus speaks, we must open our hearts. We find that when we are following Jesus, we may meet with difficult situations. He meant that by following Him we are following the truth.

Jesus did not just say it, but He showed us that He was the way, the truth, and the life; no one goes to the Father but through Jesus. When Jesus speaks of the narrow gate, He is pointing out to us that there are some restrictions when we are in the path going there because they want everyone who goes there to be perfect like them. When we follow Jesus, we are on the way to the Father. He links us to God perfectly well because He is both human and divine.

Jesus came to show us the way we should conduct our business. Whatever we do we should do it truthfully. So when we follow Him as our model, we will never go wrong. He acted in such a way that we could see the truth. We are starting to do things that are not truthful. Where would we have copied it from? Yet He is our model. If we look at it closely, the truth will always set you free. At times it appears as if things are not going well because you are saying the truth, but if you hold on to it, the right thing will always prevail. You need to be clearly convicted and be convinced that Jesus is Lord. Wherever you go wrong, you confess your sins and never repeat them; that is a sure way of preparing for eternal life.

CHAPTER 7

DEATH IS NOT THE END; THERE IS ETERNAL LIFE

If we are following Jesus, we know that we are following one who conquered death and is alive, which means we will also be alive like Him. What we have to do is to keep His Word and do His will, and we will live. Although we will face the death of this flesh, our souls will live, because we will have followed the one who is alive.

In John 5:24, Jesus is giving assurance to those who keep His words that they will have eternal life. Jesus is not promising that there will not be any problems to those who keep His words, but the promise is for getting eternal life.

When Jesus says, "Those who hear my words and keep them will not die" (see John 8:48–59), He is talking of spiritual death and not death of the flesh. When Jesus gave those words that would give us eternal life, we could not understand them. Whenever He wanted to show us divine things to help us earn salvation, because of our lack of understanding, we hate Him for that. When He speaks of not dying, He speaks of eternal life, not the dying of blood and flesh which was not what He meant. Only whenever He reveals it to us is when we can understand what He was meaning by saying that.

It is said there is eternal life in Jesus Christ, but that is not automatic, that means we have to have faith that He is the Messiah. We may be living in the same world, but at death we separate. Those who believe and nonbelievers will separate in the end, so to say death is not the end is a message for those who believe only.

LET US STRIVE TO BE PERFECT

You need to look closely to what Jesus did and said while He was still here on earth with us. That must have been proof enough and should strengthen our faith, and we should be always faithful to Him and our faith should keep on growing. Jesus's deeds and words were quite clear, but sometimes we choose to align with things that lead to destruction, because they please our flesh.

God tries by all means to show us that He loves us. He does not mean to harm us, but where He shows these signs, that is where we run away from Him. It is hard luck on our part that makes us run away from His love. His love is such that, no matter how much we forsake Him, He will still bring rain to the good and the bad, sunshine to those who love and to those who hate Him. But why is it that some hate Him? His burdens are lighter. He wants those of us who have believed in Him to be His ambassadors here on earth, so that everyone can see heaven through us. His desire is for everyone to go to heaven.

Blessed are those who hear His words and keep them, for they are on the way to eternal life. You become a faithful servant if you hear His words and obey them. That means that you will be doing what is said by the words because you have obeyed them. Doing His will means making Him happy, and you will become a child of God. To make God happy is to make

God your way of life, which means you are staying in Him and Him in you, and you are one thing. To hear the word is one thing, and to do what the word says is another. Obedience is more than sacrifice, because one who obeys will do the right thing at all times.

CHAPTER 8

RESURRECTION MEANS SALVATION TO THOSE WHO BELIEVE

Believing in Jesus means we are delivered from sin and its consequences. Know that if you are in sin, you are caught in the net of the devil, who is happy to see you go to hell and face all that happens in hell. When we are coming to Christ, we are coming for salvation, which means we are redeemed. He is called the Redeemer, who paid a ransom when the devil was putting us in his chains.

The devil was very happy to be leading us to hell, until Jesus died on the cross. His resurrection from the dead is when the devil was defeated. But still, the devil is not taking it lying down and keeps trying to lead many astray. Now he is very tactful and is employing some new methods of leading people astray and is taking many away from the path of righteousness without them knowing it.

The resurrection of Christ means salvation to those who believe. Jesus was able to remove sin and all that is attached to it, which is the penalty of sin. Believers are assured that as followers of Him who rose from the dead, they will also rise, even if they die this physical death. This is an assurance that whoever believes in Him will follow His example and will also rise again.

So His rising from the dead is at the centre of our Christianity, and we do not hesitate to tell people that they will rise again if they follow Christ and all that He laid as a foundation. When we take His word to the people, we are glad that we have something to tell them. We can give the message with complete confidence, and when we tell them they will also rise, we really mean it.

Although Jesus performed miracles, this is the most spiritual one. Our hopes are all tied to the resurrection, knowing that if we follow Christ in everything, we will also rise to life when the time comes. We know that our hopes are not in vain: the One we are emulating did it, and we will also do it, if we follow Him in truth and in spirit.

OUR HOPES WILL BE REWARDED

The problem we face is that we lack the revelation and the faith to see what happens in the remote future. To have faith in what will happen in that remote future, the best advice is to listen to the voice of the Holy Spirit. We know that our Lord promises us nothing but the truth.

The other thing we have to bear in mind is that we are running a race, in which we have to follow the rules of the game all the time. Our Lord wants us to keep the rules in order to reward us. That is where most of us are failing; we cannot keep the rules to the end. Sometimes we think it is enough to keep the rules for a season in life, and then we have done enough. Yet His rules are to be kept to the end, then you can receive the crown. The Lord cannot break His promise; He promised us that if we keep our faith, we will be rewarded.

Yes, the cross saved us from sin, but the resurrection completed the circle that was meant for our salvation.

This means Christ did it all for us. As Christians we must be happy with Easter because it brought us salvation.

How meaningful the resurrection is for us depends on what we believe about it. Sometimes it is like the story of the Sower. When he was sowing, some of the seeds fell by the wayside straight away; some birds of the earth came and picked them up. There was nothing the sower could do about it; he had done his part.

The pain that Jesus went through at Calvary was for you and me to get salvation, but then, we have to have faith that it was done for you and me. His resurrection is a miracle that we cannot run away from. They tried by all means to spread the word that He was stolen from the grave, but that lie did not go anywhere. The fact still remains that He is alive, sin has been conquered, and death has no power—but the devil does not like us to have that belief. He tries by all means to sow seeds of disbelief.

EVIL WAS DEFEATED ON THE CROSS

By staying in the Lord, we are saying that although it might seem we are losing the battle, we are following our Saviour's path. When He was dying on the cross, the devil called his angels, and they celebrated. All the forces of darkness were very happy at the cross, thinking that they had won the battle, yet they were far from it. Little did they know that on the third day they were going to get the shock of their lives because that meant the defeat of evil forever. That meant the crushing of the serpent's head (see Genesis 3:15). Although they tried to cover by giving soldiers a lot of money and told them to spread the story that the disciples had stolen him during their sleep, how could they sleep on watch? All their plans to cover it up it didn't work.

This should be a good lesson to Christians. When we might feel that God has abandoned us, the reverse is the truth. We must not expect God to treat us with soft hands and start treating us differently. If He did it to His Son, what about to us? His Son even asked why His Father had forsaken Him, yet He was not forsaken; that is how God works.

We were not promised that we would not meet hardships on this earth, but this story of Jesus must teach us that He has not abandoned us but loves us in all circumstances. He did it to His Son as a way of defeating evil; He can still do the same to us because we are not spared. When that happens to us, let us grow in our faith, knowing that those forces of evil were happy at the cross but were shocked on the third day.

When they were being washed away, they were desperate enough to cling to a straw, spreading a naked lie that "He was stolen while we were asleep." Is that lie that was spread still valid to this day? No one is confirming that for sure He was stolen, but what is spreading today is that He is now seated at the right-hand side of the Father. By conquering both evil and death, Jesus made it possible for us to be saved. If we put our trust and faith in Him, that means He is able to keep those things away from us.

The death of Christ and His resurrection can be taken as a single process for the salvation of man. Before Jesus came people offered animals as a sacrifice, the blood of animals so that God would pardon them. Today, because of the Holy Spirit who was promised us, He came and now dwells in us. His work is to reveal to us what we would not know before the coming of the Holy Spirit.

CHRIST IS ALIVE TODAY AND FOR EVERMORE

The devil was confident that what had happened in the garden of Eden was repeating itself again at Golgotha.

This the devil thought without knowing that this was truly the reversal of the garden of Eden. This time the devil was left speechless, because all his schemes had failed; it was a very good sign that he and his followers were heading for hell.

The author is reminding the reader that we are at a crossroads: let us choose now whom to follow and what to do to be saved. The time to do that is now. Always in life, people seem to want to identify themselves with successful people, even if there is no way they can benefit from that. But here, if we associate ourselves with this Man, we gain an eternal benefit: because He defeated death, that means we will also defeat death if we follow Him. He is eternity, we will have eternal life if we follow Him. He was resurrected from death, which means our souls will have a resurrection if we follow Him.

All we are doing is striving for the resurrection of our souls. Jesus is being very kind to us because He is offering to share His victory with us. What He did was for our good because of His love to us; we have to respond to that extended hand of friendship. We are reminded at the resurrection that death came through humanity; now salvation has come through a man but this time as a result of the resurrection of that man. This was done so that everyone might be saved.

This death of Christ had a single purpose: for you and me to be saved. All that Jesus suffered for was so that we might obtain salvation. We should take this salvation seriously because it came about through someone's pain. That is the greatest miracle that was ever performed, when Jesus triumphed over death. We are also going to triumph over death if we follow Him—that is, having faith in Him. As He lives, we are also assured of living also if we follow Him faithfully. Jesus leads the way in everything, and we are His followers, which means as He triumphed over death, we will also triumph over our death. As He is living, we will also live.

CHAPTER 9

JESUS IS THE RESURRECTION AND THE LIFE

When we talk of the resurrection, we are talking about Christ because there is no other resurrection than in Christ. When we talk of the resurrection of the soul, we are talking of the soul that is in Christ, because there is no resurrection of the soul that is not in Christ. The resurrection is important because it spelled defeat for death and sin and because it is a pillar of Christianity. All Christians are empowered to convince the world to follow Christianity because of the resurrection.

Christians are able to say, "Come to Christianity," because they have something to offer, and are able to say with confidence there will be a resurrection of souls in the end because we are following in the footsteps of Christ. They have strong assurance of that because Christ said He was the resurrection and the life. We all strive to avoid death, but it still comes without us liking it, having failed to avoid it, we have to say. But we have something on offer: someone offering us the resurrection and giving us our life back. So we have to take the offer and all the goodness in that offer. "I am the resurrection and the life." By this He means He can give us our lives back, and we can live again.

God is true and honest to us, that is the reason why He made his Son to have a human nature so that He would feel the same as we feel. If it were not like that, we might have said, "He asks us to do difficult things because He does not feel what we feel." But now we have no escape route because we are walking the route that He walked.

The way God chooses to do His thing is different from the way we think, God made Jesus to walk a very difficult path, being beaten and nailed on the cross, bleeding as if God were not there. Yet that is the way He showed His love to us. If at all we were going to have that same sacrificial love as His, we would change the world. He did it to show us and expects us to do the same. He does not expect anything less from us. If we earnestly follow Him, it will only be a matter of time until we will also be raised to life, as He does not break His promise. His promise is to make us rise again if we follow Him both in deeds and in spirit. Because God is Spirit, anyone who comes to Him must do it in the spirit also. As per His promise, if we follow Him, He will lead us through the path that leads to eternal life. Let us all think deeply about what life means and what it is to us. We all want life; that is why the author is pleading with the reader to strive for eternal life. Nothing less will be good for us.

DEATH WAS DEFEATED AT THE RESURRECTION

When Jesus said He was the resurrection and the life, He meant that those who have faith in Him will have a resurrection of their souls. That means those who believe will share His triumph over death. The worst thing we can suffer is to die the second death of our souls. The importance of the resurrection is that it shows the power of God over death; when we follow Him, we will also have power over death.

We must trust that He created us in His own image, and He is responsible for our lives if we put our trust in Him. Jesus was mostly misunderstood by the Pharisees because while he was speaking spiritually, they were speaking in the flesh. That is why the author is appealing with the reader to always worship Him in truth and in spirit (John 4:23). Jesus has power to make us live. Although our fleshly bodies may die, surely He can make us live a spiritual life which leads to eternity as a result of believing in Him. Jesus's words should not be taken out of context, because He did not mean this flesh will not die. No, this flesh may perish, but if the soul believes that Jesus is the Messiah, then that soul has life in it. This world was condemned to death because of the devil's lies because the devil wants to see us die in our sins, but Jesus came to redeem it from the lies of the devil.

Let us talk to God in prayer. He is faithful; He will give us the divine revelation that can enable us to change the world. Jesus did not mince His words and did not hesitate to say that I might offend some people who might not love Him. He said words just as we should pass them along. For instance, we can say that no one goes to the Father but through Him; what a promise! If it were up to us, we might hesitate to say that, but it is a fact of life that there is no salvation in any other.

We ask the Lord to give us the courage to preach the gospel as it should be. The interesting reality is that Jesus does not say anything about which He did not also set an example. When He says you will rise again, He demonstrated it by rising up Himself. He even said, "If you can only believe, you will live" (see John 11:25–26). Let us believe in Him; He will not forsake us. He is faithful, and let us be faithful to His promise. Because He rose from the dead, if we believe in Him, that means we will also rise as well and live as He lives. To live in Christ means living a spiritual life, meaning eternal life.

CHAPTER 10

WHY DO WE CELEBRATE EASTER?

Christians are of a strong belief that Jesus really rose from the dead and is alive—that this is the biggest spiritual miracle that ever happened. Some miracles came and went, but this one is there always, so Christians are happy to keep on remembering this day.

There is a day each year set aside to remember this day of Christ's resurrection. Not only do Christians see it as a miracle; they see it as the coming of salvation. Humanity was condemned to hell, but through Jesus's blood we have been ransomed and redeemed. That is why we should celebrate this Easter Day. It is time to examine this in depth, even to many who have never put a thought to it.

We should reflect on one surprising part of Easter is that even those who claim not to want to believe that Christ exists will still celebrate. They do not want to be reminded that it is for Christ; they just want to celebrate it quietly as if it had no connection with the death and resurrection of Jesus. The children want to celebrate more than the older ones; they may be taking it from where Jesus said, "Let the children come to me, for the kingdom of is for those who are like the little children."

FORTY DAYS AFTER THE RESURRECTION

Jesus chose to stay on earth forty days after His resurrection, for He wanted to prove to people beyond any doubt that He was alive. Still, some doubt, saying that it was just a delusion. It is up to us to ask for a revelation because without the revelation we may go on and on, holding on the wrong issue. The day when Jesus was nailed to the cross, instead of people crying, they call it Good Friday, meaning that it was good that blood was flowing on the cross for us to be saved. This is where it is surprising that even those who do not believe in Christ still call it Good Friday.

This is the time when God's plans came to the climax

and had come to the planned conclusion. Some forces never wanted the plan to work, because those forces never wanted us to be redeemed, but the light prevailed against darkness; the will of God worked and was done. At the resurrection is where death was defeated, and all the devil's plans came to nought (came to zero). All Christians have every reason to celebrate because the plan of God to buy us back by the blood of Jesus had worked; everything had gone according to plan.

His resurrection has proved to be the crowning miracle. It could not be imagined by those who do not believe, but to the believers it signifies that their souls will also have a resurrection in the end. If you are a believer, you have to receive this as good news. We can excuse Christians when they say Good Friday when someone is being crucified. They are saying, even though Jesus suffered the pain, we agree that He suffered for our sake. The pain and the resurrection have made the way for Christians to be resurrected also, so the crucifixion was done for our good. So we have to say Good Friday because everything was done for our good, and we received salvation because of that.

If we do not celebrate Easter, it will be simply not knowing on our part or not taking it into full consideration. God did His planning for years and did His things according to plan and worked towards fulfilling that plan. It is up to us to follow that plan because it was done for us and for our salvation

Easter is celebrated by Christians as a joyous holiday because it represents the fulfilment of prophecies of the Old Testament and the revelation of God's salvific plan for all humankind. In commemorating the resurrection of Jesus Christ, Easter also celebrates the defeat of death and hope for salvation. Christians around the world celebrate Easter to remember the resurrection of Jesus from the dead.

LET US ACCEPT JESUS AS OUR PERSONAL SAVIOUR

To learn more about Jesus's death and resurrection provided for our salvation please read the following article. What does it mean to accept Jesus as your personal Saviour?

I have to accept Jesus as my personal Saviour because when I was trapped in sin, He saved me because this sin was going to result in eternal punishment. Now I have that faith that He saved us by His grace. He died and rose again from the dead just to pay the price of my sin.

A saviour is someone who saves someone or something from danger of ruin or defeat.

We have got to learn about Jesus and know that what He went through until He died was to save you and me from our sins.

We have to take it to ourselves that when nails have gone through our hands and other nails through our feet, and the whole weight of the body is suspended there, because all parts of the body work in coordination, how will we breathe? It is not possible to change sides, as when one is free. When one is nailed to the cross, there is no voluntary movement of the body.

Christian, imagine this pain was all for your salvation, and no other person is able to help you relieve this pain. "God give us a heart" we may fail to help, but we must give glory for all the pain He went through for us.

We are considering "excruciating" pain (intensely painful; very embarrassing, awkward, and tedious) (see Matthew 27:46). This pain was not for five minutes, not for thirty minutes, but from nine in the morning until three o'clock p.m. He was bearing my weight upon Himself. Imagine, if the pain is too much on the wrist or the hands, the muscles may break, causing the weight to be on the feet. If they cannot bear the weight, but they have no means of changing, that will mean the whole weight of the body is crushing down on itself, causing shortness of breath because the lungs are compressed. The blood vessels are compressed, causing deprivation of oxygen supply to other parts of the body. No relief is coming from anywhere nothing to relieve any pain from anywhere. You will not wonder when He calls out, "My God, my God, why have you forsaken me?" The pain was at its highest, all for you and me.

CHAPTER 11

JESUS' RESURRECTION MEANS SALVATION AND ETERNAL LIFE FOR ALL BELIEVERS

We were destined for hell, but the love of Jesus was to suffer those pains, for us to have salvation. That means our salvation was bought by very precious blood. In response we must give all the glory to Him because He deserves it. Our hopes for eternal life are pinned on those pains which He experienced because of love for us. Let us take the resurrection of Christ as meaning eternal life for us. The problem we face is that we want something tangible today, not to be promised eternal life later. To us, this appears to be very remote.

If there was no resurrection, all that Jesus suffered on the cross would have been in vain. Now that He did all that for us, we have become new creations who are capable of death and resurrection as well. This is what our Saviour demonstrated. When we die, let us die with Christ, and let us rise with Christ. By that we mean anyone who dies in Christ will rise again because Christ rose from the dead and is alive.

All that was God's plan for Jesus to suffer on the cross, and the plan was that He would rise again. He did as per God's plan, and this was accomplished because everything went according to how it was planned (Romans 6:8–11). Here Paul is saying that by the death of Jesus it means He died with our sins, and when He rises up with our souls into glory, Paul wants us to be happy but not to sin purposely (2 Corinthians 5:17). In our lives we must count on the resurrection because this brought us happiness and joy—not the joy that ends, but everlasting Joy because that means we will die once but live forever. Presently we have hope, and for the future we have hope.

We have to remind each other the resurrection came as God's grace. He put all our curse and punishment on the cross. The resurrection of Jesus was the greatest miracle because no one can tell how the tombstone was rolled off and how the headcloth was folded nicely and for what reason. If it means Jesus is coming again, why don't we believe in His second coming? And let us be on our guard so as not to be taken unawares, since we have seen all the warning signs.

Jesus is eternity. "Now this is eternal life: that they know you, the only true God, and Jesus Christ, whom you have sent" (John 17:3 NIV). This gives us a simple calculation: if Jesus says, "Be in Me, and I will be in you," and if He is in the Father, that will mean that our relationship with the Trinity will be interwoven. That clarifies that if they are eternity, that means we will have eternal life. This has to be borne in mind: the Trinity is holy. For us to qualify, we have to confess our sins in order to be holy like them.

Eternity is unaccountable existence without end. Sometimes we tend to think of eternity as only meaning never-ending life, yet there is also eternal punishment for an infinite time. Forever is an extremely long time—infinite time, lasting throughout eternity. There is also in the programmes of computing a loop that goes on and on, following one after the other. Eternity means forever; it looks like a time that will never end. People who promise to love one another for eternity are planning not to ever split up. That means they are going to stay together all their lives without separation.

CHAPTER 12

PENTECOSTAL WAY OF SALVATION

Pentecostals want to search deeper into the Scriptures. Pentecostals are all about wanting to know it for themselves; that means they are eager to learn. Their belief is that all Scriptures are inspired by God. Their desire to search deeper into the Scriptures bears fruit. Their eagerness is manifested in their deeds, and they expect also to get a clear revelation.

They believe that if you walk in the forest regularly, one day you will find there is a way. This means that their beliefs could be right. That is why they keep on searching the Scriptures; it pays dividends in the end. They expect their interpretation to be well guided by the Holy Spirit.

Every believer in Christ is to be a part of the body of Christ. They believe that, as promised by Christ, the Holy Spirit will be with you all the time: that is, if you seek the Holy Spirit, He will be on you. They believe in the church, through baptism, but they do not believe in the Trinity. The Bible teaches that we cannot be saved by our works, but by grace alone. We should have faith and believe that He is merciful. The whole reason why God sent His Son into the world is because He is merciful to us. Lord, you can help us to be faithful enough for You to save us.

Pentecostalism is a form of Christianity that believes on the work of the Holy Spirit in people. The work of the Holy Spirit in people is to take away from us what is not godly and put in what is godly, so our characters become pleasing to God. The reason why we say we cannot be saved by our works but by faith is because of His love and mercy, and the effect of the Holy Spirit will now depend on how each individual is filled. The way the Holy Spirit fills us is like the human being growing from childhood to an adult; hence the Holy Spirit fills us gradually until we feel the spirit moving in our hearts.

WHY SHOULD WE SEARCH THE SCRIPTURES?

The Scripture is our free consultant, the reason being that the Lord Himself inspired these Scriptures to be made. The purpose was to make everyone aware of what He wants His people to know, because He is very concerned that His people should have some knowledge. In other words, the Lord knows that if His people have knowledge, they will grow spiritually. It is a fact that if we search the Scripture with a desire to learn, the Lord Himself will reveal them to us because He wants us to know Him, and His ways, and to know the relationship that is there between God and humanity.

Our aim is to return home where we came from, so when we search the Scriptures, we are navigating our way home. By searching the Scriptures, we will get to know the truth about Him and His ways. We must remember that where we are trying to find His truth, the devil is also sowing seeds of disbelief to try to take us away from the right path. If your journey is against the direction of the wind, that means you are faced with difficulties that threaten to divert you from your destination. To reach your destination, you have to employ some techniques. It is not enough to know the truth of God without putting it into practice and making it your life application, which means you are practising what you say. Saying something is one thing; doing it is another. To know the truth about God acknowledges that it all has to be learned, like any other modern technique. It is not just taking it in without knowing which methods to apply to it. You will need all the requirements of it.

To know the Scriptures, we have to apply a loving approach; that is, to love the truth in it, so that it will be of some help to us now and in future.

Pentecostals believe that faith must be powerfully experiential. Faith is not cultural or ritual, but must be felt by an individual, not like a shared communal experience but one given us as individuals—and it is not automatic. It is not a matter of performing rituals but of feeling the spirit moving in you.

They believe in the resurrection of the soul in the end. The resurrection is not something that is done in groups but depends on how divine your soul is, so the advice of the author to the reader is that we must work for the divinity of our souls, so that in the end there is a resurrection. Believing in the resurrection of Christ is thinking that if we follow Him, our souls will also be resurrected as Jesus has already shown the way of how we can be saved. If we reflect and see how we have offended the Lord, and we repent, we can be forgiven our sins and be admitted into the family of God.

Pentecostals believe in both a literal heaven and hell. The heaven is for those who have accepted God's gift of salvation, while hell is for those who have rejected the gift of salvation. For Pentecostals, there is no other requirement to salvation. The Baptists believe that being saved is something that happens once in a person's life and that it lasts forever. Their belief is that once a person accepts Jesus as their Saviour, they will never again be at risk of going to hell. On the other hand, Pentecostals believe that one can lose salvation if the faith is not kept. That means their thinking and belief is different from the Baptists. The point is that a person should have to lead a sinless life even after being saved.

HOW TO LIVE A SINLESS LIFE

Jesus's mission on earth was to set an example that we would follow; hence we are following the footsteps of Jesus. Jesus lived a perfect, sinless life so if that is what we are emulating, what are we doing to also live a sinless life? When Jesus came to earth, He was representing the heavenly kingdom. When He left, He left everything in our care, meaning that whatever He did, we are the ones who have to carry it on, knowing that we have to accept the responsibility for whatever goes wrong. For example, when He said, "Go therefore and teach all nations" (see Matthew 28:19), He meant that He would not be there but it was us representing Him. He even mentioned that He would be with us, meaning that we are representing Him fully.

This makes us realise that we are carrying some responsibilities of being ambassadors of the heavenly kingdom, where only the holy ones live. How are we going to qualify if we live a sinful life? We must pray and strive to live a sinless life. If we look at life today, we all know what is sin or what can lead us into sin, but we tend to try to ignore it, or to have the attitude that God will compromise. Yet we very well know that God cannot be bribed into doing what we want Him to do, because God never changes. It is we who have to change our habits of doing things and do what He wants us to do. If we do that, it means we are abiding by His laws, which pleases Him.

We must always pray and desire to live a sinless

life not corrupted by this world. We are living in a corrupted world where the forces in it are striving to corrupt us. It makes all things in it very attractive, in order to lure us into accepting them; if we do, then we are in it. If these things manage to attract us and strain our relationship with God, it is because our desire for purity is spoiled. We are no purer in the eyes of God, because we have not obeyed Him and have chosen to take our own ways, which are not His ways.

We know that because of original sin, we have all drifted from our Creator, but there is one who was very sympathetic of us and redeemed us. We are no longer bound by original sin; He has made a new covenant with us which makes us qualified to be called the sons and daughters of the Highest. Sometimes we get into situations where Jesus is calling us to follow Him, but we find ourselves turning the other way, because of the love of this corrupt world. We forget that there is something we are pursuing which can perish within a day. O Lord, we ask You to give us wisdom, because we perish because for the lack of it.

Let us always pray that God makes us sinless people. That is possible if our relationship is sound and perfect, and we need to stay close to Him because He is perfect.

We can also be perfect like Him; there is nothing to stop us if we only obey all what we are required to do to stay pure. He can set us apart—that is, sanctify us—and make us pure always, His sacred religious people of whom he is proud.

CHAPTER 13

THE GREATNESS OF JESUS CHRIST

The uniqueness of Jesus is that even though He took human form, He was conceived of the spirit. We Christians are encouraged to know that we are following a unique person who is both shepherd and saviour; in believing that, we also find help for ourselves. When the angel met Mary to tell her that she was blessed, He also mentioned that Jesus would be great, so that means His greatness was also God's plan of salvation.

Christ is God and man in person, The way He was born and the way He lived His life were unique. He is very special in that our lives depend on Him. It is advisable to follow Him, for following Him leads to eternal life. During His life on earth, He performed miracles which are beyond any doubt. The new covenant that He made with us will last forever.

His greatness is already demonstrated when He says all authority is given unto Him from heaven and earth (see Matthew 28:18). This means without Him nothing on earth can exist, and all the glory must be to Him. John the Baptist acknowledged His greatness by saying he was unfit even to untie or tie His shoes. His greatness is also in His titles—for instance, "the Son of the Highest."

John is unique in his message that with a distinctive emphasis, believers find an ongoing source of expanding their concept of the Saviour's greatness. Jesus Christ is greater than the greatest of the prophets of both the Old Testament and New Testament. In the past God used to speak to us through the prophets, but lastly, He spoke to us through His Son Jesus Christ, and now He is speaking to us through the Holy Spirit.

What the people say about Him ranges very widely: Prophet, Priest, Saviour, Shepherd, Lord, King, Messiah. What confirms it all is that all authority from heaven and on earth is in his hands. The good with Jesus is that He does not hold it to Himself but He imparted it to us.

We must not pride ourselves about it but rather take it seriously, that we have to represent Him here on earth, where He expects us to act as His ambassadors.

JESUS, YESTERDAY, TODAY, AND TOMORROW

Jesus is right by being the same as He was yesterday. That is still how he is today, and He will still be the same tomorrow. Sometimes we want Him to do things our own way. We are people of various opinions; what I want is not what my neighbour wants, so how is Jesus going to get along with us that way? The only way is for us to follow His ways, which will try to accommodate everyone.

Hebrews tells us that Jesus never changes . In that way, He becomes just to everybody. He is faithful to everyone, and not only faithful but loving to everyone. That is why we say, He was like that yesterday, He is like that today, and He will be like that tomorrow.

We are to keep on praying so that we are kept away from the love of this world. That is the best we can do to stay close to Him who is surrounded by glorious things. All things around Him are glittering; that is what we are also longing for. We strive to stay close to Him because we have to be content with what He has.

Everything on earth is His, so those things will be ours if we follow Him to the very end. We are urged to put all our trust in the Lord because He will not fail us. If we put our trust in humans, one day they change and we are left in the cold without any protection.

What we must all realise is that Jesus's power is not history. It was like that yesterday; we can see His power working today, and it will still be working like that tomorrow. That means, Jesus's power must be felt or seen today and continue for the time to come and for evermore. Sometimes we do forget: what is happening today may have happened before and still may happen again in the future. He makes His plans well in advance and warns us.

Let us remember that we have the Holy Spirit to guide us all the time and to warn us of the future. We must obey the Holy Spirit so that our relationship with God will be a good relationship. What happens with us is that we change ourselves, and we expect the Holy Spirit to change also.

GOD NEVER CHANGES, BUT MAN CHANGES:

God's attributes never change, God will never change. What He plans for generations will never change; it will happen according to plan. What we have to do is to understand Him, and it is for us to follow His ways, not to try to make Him follow our way. That is where we go against Him sometimes. Instead of understanding Him and doing His will, we try to make Him do things our own way, which is impossible and will not happen. Sometimes because of the shortness of our minds we tend to think that there are times He changed His plans, but a closer look shows that it is not like that.

We want God to change with us, forgetting that God is for all. It is we who must come to Him and have relations with Him. His love to us never falters or wavers. He made the Scriptures to warn us. He inspired them to be there for us. Let us obey those Scriptures because they are there to give us relationship with God (Ephesians 1:18–19). We have a feeling in ourselves that He will not let us down. We are quite certain of our future, knowing that the Holy Spirit is with us all the time of our lives. The world fears some man-made powers such as atomic power without realising that there is power vested in us by Him who has power over death. That is why we who believe in Him should be contented that we have the power.

THE GREATEST POWER IS INVESTED IN US THROUGH THE RESURRECTION

We should value our relationship with Christ as more important than anything else (see Philippians 3:7–11). It is important for us to look closely and find that everything Christ went through was for our gain, knowing that we will obtain resurrecting as He did. Christ Himself pleaded with us to take his yoke upon us and learn His ways. For our relationship with Him to be a sound relationship, we must leave some of our ways of doing things and follow His ways. To inherit someone's property, you must have some relationship with that person. For us to inherit from Christ, we must have some relationship with Him, and for that, we must do things that please Him. Having a good relationship with Him means seeking Him every day and talking to Him very often.

When we talk of our resurrection, it means we are being like Him. Yet to be like Him, we have to give up some of the things that please our flesh. This involves a great deal of sacrifice, which in turn means a great joy tomorrow. Indeed, there will be great joy at the resurrection of our souls.

When we are making our schedules, we must do so in such a way that we will be able to accommodate Christ. Sometimes we find that we will be living for Him. The good thing with Christ is that when we strive, He will give us His power. He will not leave us comfortless; sometimes we have not to worry but only to do things that please Him. We must know Him and do His will, and He will do the rest.

If somehow there were no resurrection, what would we preach to the people? Now that there is resurrection, people are going to be convinced that He is alive and that He intercedes between us and the Father. Everyone knows that He is the most powerful in heaven and on earth. All we are doing by following Him is to have power like He has; He promised to impart that power to us if we follow Him (see Acts 1:8).

The greatest power that is invested in us is the power of resurrection, which is the greatest of all powers. What we must ask for while we are still on earth is for Him to give us the power to fight against all temptations that might want to sway us from the Lord and all the eternity that He has prepared for us. With Him, in all our struggles of life we will become victorious. Whenever there are some failures in our lives, He helps us. We can rise again, and He gives us strength to continue with the life as it is meant for us and prepared for us. We will see it through with His grace, and He will help us to do the rest.

CHAPTER 14

WHAT CHRISTIANS BELIEVE AND FOLLOW

Christians believe in God the Father, Jesus Christ as the Son of God, and the Holy Spirit as the intercessor. Christianity is an Abrahamic, monotheistic religion, worshipping one God and denying all other gods. This religion has about 2.5 billion followers.

Christians believe that since Jesus was fully human and wholly divine, He really died, was buried, stayed in the grave for three days, and rose on the third day. All this had been preplanned and went according to plan. Jesus was born of a virgin Mary and became a human being; this was done in order for the people to be believed. After Jesus had gone to heaven and people on this earth could be preaching, they could be believed because even Jesus Himself became human.

Christians believe that they have inherited all that Jesus commissioned to his disciples when he was going. Now that the apostles have also gone, we have now inherited their charge. Whatever the apostles were tasked to do is now our responsibility to carry out—and to do it as Jesus required it to be done. Jesus went through all the stages of life because He was fully human. He experienced every stage of life, so He fully understands our needs.

He gave us a very good example of how life should be lived. He loved the oppressed, the widows, the orphans, the outcast. and those who were looked down upon. He wants us to follow that example and carry on where He left off. That is a real assignment, and He expects that at His second coming we will give a report without hesitation, because we will have honestly carried out our assignment.

THE ACTS OF THE APOSTLES HAVE SINCE BEEN PASSED ON TO US

Jesus was born in a Jewish family, but the church today has moved from Judaism to be the church of the Gentiles. It is pleasing to note that the acts of the apostles have passed it on to us. The church today is teaching people to follow Jesus, not to follow a religion. The apostles were teaching people to follow Jesus's example, which is what the church is doing today to teach people about the true God who sent His Son into the world so that the world should not perish, not a religion.

Those acts of the apostles spread all over the world with an alarming speed. Immediately after the ascension of Jesus into heaven is when the apostles started going all over spreading the gospel—now without their earlier fear. That is why today we say, let us ask for divine power to be able to spread the word without fear, because those forces of persecution against the early apostles are still alive and are still with us, using every means they can to make the gospel fail.

When we say that the acts of the apostles have been passed on to us, we mean everything that was happening those days is happening to us today; as individuals we are not spared at all. From the Abrahamic covenant to the New Covenant of Jesus, we are now guided with the Holy Spirit in all the days of our lives. We must be glad today that we are under the guidance of the Holy Spirit, who will not fail us. Without being selective, the Holy Spirit can be received by anyone, Gentile or Jew.

When Jesus said all power was given to Him in heaven and on earth, He imparted this power to the disciples, which is in turn passed down to us. So let us use this power, knowing that He has done it in order for His work to be carried out. We must give thanks to Luke, a gentile who, some two thousand years ago, thought of this generation. Now we are enlightened because of him. We now have the baton in our hand, to relay it on to the next generation, expecting them to receive it from us in good shape.

Jesus taught or commissioned His disciples. For example, in Luke 11:1–4, He taught His disciples to follow a model prayer. This is not to say that they should repeat the same words, but to say when they come to pray, they should not bring a shopping list. When they come to Him, they should know that their Father loved them before they did. So when they come to Him, they are coming to have a conversation with their Father, who knows all their problems. He is not trying to make them unhappy, but He wants to see them living a better life. He taught them the Lord's Prayer, which has since been passed on to us, and many other things.

What the Lord did through the apostles is done by all Christians today; if not, they are doing something like it. We are being reminded here that the apostles' responsibility after the ascension of Jesus has been passed on to us; there is no doubt about that because we have seen the example.

CHRISTIANS BELIEVE IN THE TRINITY

Christians believe in God the Father, Jesus Christ the Son, and the Holy Spirit and in the death, descent into hell, resurrection, and ascension of Christ, and in the holiness of the church and the communion of saints, and in Christ's second coming, the day of judgement, and the salvation of the faithful.

In order for Jesus to be able to give us an example, He had to be like us by taking on human nature. At the same time, He had to preserve His divinity. To receive salvation, Christians have to follow in Jesus's footsteps because that is what is expected of them, to believe all that He said and put into practice all that He taught. We are also expected to be exemplary to those who follow us.

His teachings were to let us know what God wants from us. If we do it willingly, He is inviting us to the godly family, and we must now understand that he is king of the heavenly kingdom. If we do that, we become

His children. His teaching and his growing popularity did not go over well with the rulers. who, without a revelation, thought it to be a political popularity. Yet they misunderstood that His kingship was not of this world but of the heavenly kingdom leading to eternity. With that misunderstanding, He was crucified in order to get rid of that popularity. To this date we may be mixing the heavenly kingdom with the earthly kingdom. These are two separate kingdoms, and they are miles apart.

Jesus died and was buried, but on the third day He rose from the dead. He did all this for our sins: His dying on the cross, His burial, and His rising from the dead were all God's plan of salvation. This has demonstrated that following Him leads to eternity. We are required to hear His words and do them; this will lead to eternity. Following all that He said and did means that we are doing the will of God, which will lead us to everlasting life.

WE ARE TO DO THE WILL OF GOD

We all know what are God's requirements. We need to stay strong to be able to abide by His Word. All that God wants is clearly explained in the Bible. We need divine guidance and divine protection in order to be able to do His will. It is said that on the cross when Jesus died, "the will of God was done." This means whatever happens in our lives is the will of God, but sometimes when we face hardships in life, we may start thinking that it is not the will of God.

To see whether we are doing the will of God or not, Jesus did all He could to set an example for us to follow. But sometimes, my friend, we may be hesitant to do exactly as He did, because all that pain He suffered on the cross was for you and me. Are we doing that for our neighbours? It may appear very difficult, but let us ask Him to give us the courage. On our own we may not be able to, but with His help we will be able to. We know that without His help, even if we wanted to give our bodies as a sacrifice (see Romans 12:1), we may not be able to unless we ask Him to help us.

It may appear to be very difficult, but if we are to be like Him, we have to ask for His help because on our own we may not be able to make it, but with His divine help we can make it. He sacrificed His body for us to obtain salvation. We do the same if we are to be like Him; we can start by showing love to one another and praying for one another. Jesus prayed for us and is still an intercessor between God and us today. As a start, we must learn to share what we have earned by using sweat to share with others, and we keep on following those lines until we come to a stage where we will be as Christ gave us the example.

The first thing is to give ourselves to God, saying, "Use me the way You find will promote Your kingdom," and He will give us the necessary guidance. There are many ways God can use us in His vineyard. Love your neighbours; start by sharing with them, paving the way with cheerful greetings. Learn to do everything in common, and you will see that you will get a good response from them.

If we look around us, we see that worldly things are all around us. Most of them are very attractive; indeed, they may become irresistible. So our hope is only in our Saviour to help us to overcome that temptation, which would cause us to drift away from His glory.

Obeying His commandments means we are doing the will of God. This will also make us grow in understanding all that shows us that God's plan of salvation has worked. All that God did to have His Son come to the earth and be like a human being—to be born in a normal way and go all through the stages of a human being until He was thirty years old—was His plan of salvation to humankind. From the very beginning, at the fall into sin, God formulated a plan for humanity's salvation. Jesus's death on the cross was very painful; He suffered the pain in order to carry our sins. He suffered a lot on the cross until He died, but the resurrection was a symbol for the resurrection of our souls. Human beings choose to follow Him or not to follow Him, but in spite of all that, He will still be on His throne. Instead we should ask for His guidance and the revelation of the kingdom to us so that by following in the right direction we can be saved by His grace.

JESUS CARRIED OUR SINS ON THE CROSS

It is very interesting to note that all what happened on the cross was done for us to get salvation (see 1 Peter 2:24). When Jesus said, "Whoever wants to be my disciple must carry his cross and follow me" (see Luke 9:23), He clearly meant that whatever hardship we might experience, He experienced it on our behalf. We should not forget such love, of someone who chooses to die in someone's place. This teaches us that whatever we meet in life is not the first hardship, because Jesus went through it as well, so it is not something unique to us alone.

Colossians 2:14 tells us that everything He suffered on the cross was to ransom us from where we were imprisoned by the devil, to redeem us. To be nailed on the cross was the most painful death which was reserved for the worst criminals, so they classified Jesus that way. Yet we were the worst criminals. He was a living sacrifice for us, and He expects us to do the same for others, but the corrupt world wants us to be afraid of doing what Jesus did.

We as Christians would be advised to learn to recognise such love as to bear our sins, as painful as it was on the cross, but He persevered in order to set us free. If someone did that on our own behalf, surely we have to show some appreciation and give all the glory to Him. That will make our relationship a brotherly relationship. What is surprising is that we want to pretend as if nothing was done for us at all, and we keep on indulging in sins as if no one ever paid for those sins. God accepted that payment, which was paid in blood because, that was according to His plan of salvation of humanity.

CHAPTER 15

JESUS COMMISSIONED HIS DISCIPLES BEFORE LEAVING

After the resurrection Jesus asked His disciples to meet Him in Galilee where he was giving the final words (see Matthew 28:16–20), in which He was asking them not to only concentrate among the Jews. This time they were to go all over the world.

In order for us to win their souls, we must be exemplary Christians—to stay pure ourselves and to pray for those we would like to convert. They will be happy to know that we pray for them; then we will have made our task easy to win their hearts to Christ, because that is what Christ is looking for from us to work in His vineyard. When we do what Jesus commanded us to do, we will be harvesting souls, which is what He was referring to in John 4:35. That is what He wants to see done because He tells us that the fields are ripe ready for harvest. We must be prepared wherever we to make the word of God known to whoever is there. Do not wait for those you know or your relatives; time is not on our side.

JESUS WANTS US TO WIN THE SOULS OF THE PEOPLE

When we are trying to win souls, are we to liken ourselves with the world? To win the souls is to try to let the world know about Jesus without ourselves being diluted or being carried away. We have to be careful that when we "fish" for people, we do not end up being fished ourselves.

We have to bear in mind that we are going to draw these people out from a corrupt world, where the devil is working overtime trying to get as many on his side as he can. So the followers of Jesus must be very vigilant, because we are after winning the souls, but the devil is after winning us to his side. If we win souls to Christ, that will give us confidence in our Christian life

We cannot run short of words to say to the world

because our Lord is faithful to always be with us through the Holy Spirit. As He promised us, so He does for us. We must be able to preserve this body of flesh which houses the soul so that it does not defile the soul. We can avert that if we ask for the intervention of divine power to help overcome that temptation; as we always ask, lead us not into temptation.

Make the Bible your handbook. Whatever a Christian puts on must be presentable. Also, do not hide your faith and love books, movies, and music about Christ. Even in social media, do not be ashamed to talk about Christ. When you preach, always ask for guidance because giving His word to the people should be inspired by Him because it His word to them; we are just vessels.

Jesus made a covenant with us made strong by the spilling of His blood on the cross at Calvary (see Matthew 26:28). If you are thinking of one nation as the chosen one, then you need some revelation. By doing that, you may be going against Jesus's mission because His mission was for the whole world. As the commission goes, it says teach all nations.

WE SHOULD NOT HIDE OUR FAITH

How can we hide our faith when Matthew 5:14 clearly requires us to be like a house built on a hill, which should give light to the world? There is nowhere we can run away from being the light of the world because, even if we did not want to talk about it, our deeds would betray us. There is no way we would say we do not want them to be Christians; our deeds will be a light to them. Christians have to know that it is a matter of wanting to do it. Once we accept that we are Christians, our light has to shine to the world and give light to the whole world.

God has the power to offer salvation to everyone who has faith in Him, regardless of whether they are Jews or Gentiles; salvation is for everyone. If you are finding it difficult to love all nations, you must ask for His divine hand to help you because He said, "I am with you always, to the very end of the age" (Matthew 28:20 NIV). So we are not alone when doing His work in His vineyard; we have no fear because we rely on His promise, for Jesus never fails.

Jesus has not stopped giving us instructions to make more disciples because He wants everyone to be in the fold. Jesus's mission on earth was to introduce the heavenly kingdom so that everyone who believes and follows it may be saved from the second death. He came for the poor and the oppressed, so that they may be set free; the blind will see, and those who are in the chains of Satan will be set free.

WE ARE REQUIRED TO PREACH WHAT WE DO

We Christians have a big task ahead of us because we have a task to discipline ourselves first so that we can preach by our deeds. He is not only asking us to do it, but He himself did it. The Pharisees used to make laws for others to follow which they themselves could not follow, and Jesus was always against that

As the disciples were working to spread the gospel through the world, they were obeying this instruction from the Great Commission, which we must also obey. Jesus gave instructions to His disciples which is popularly known as the Great Commission, to go and teach all nations so that everyone would know of the heavenly kingdom. He put some emphasis on baptising them with the Holy Spirit, as He had promised that He would send the Holy Spirit to be with us all our lives, guiding us and letting us know all about God. Spreading the gospel throughout the world is everyone's task, as we are going to answer these questions on the judgement day.

As Christians, we are all called to carry out this by following His instructions. We follow them by bringing the heavenly kingdom to the people, which started with Jesus. When He was leaving, He commissioned His disciples to take it up where He left off. Now it is like a relay; the disciples have handed it down to us. Now that Great Commission is on us, and we are to go and teach all nations.

As we are carrying out His work throughout the whole world, Jesus wants all souls to be saved, and He has put that task on us to ensure that the gospel reaches everyone. As He gave the disciples instructions to go to everyone, He warned them not to leave Jerusalem without being clothed with the Holy Spirit, because the Holy Spit will give us what to say and what to do so that we do not mislead people by giving them the wrong doctrine.

CHRISTIANITY IS BEING GIVEN A CHOICE

Christian life is to be directed and guided by the Lord. Our Christian way must always be lit by Him. Where we are about to get into problems, He leads us away from them in order to save our souls. Everything we do and say is all guided by Him, and we are walking in a well-lit path.

The biggest trap that is within us that we have to make a choice between following Christ or the devil, but in most cases, we are found following the devil because his ways please our flesh. To try to avoid this, we must try to make ourselves live a religious life, like some who may choose to be priests or pastors. To live a religious life is to let Christ live in you, so that whatever you do is guided by the Holy Spirit, who will be doing everything for you. You will be leading a Christian life. You will be living by faith; everything you do will no longer be you, but it will be Christ who will be living in you. If we are living the life according to what He wants, we will be living life to its fullest.

People of Old Testament times used to sacrifice animals, but God says sacrificing yourself by obeying His instructions and doing His will is better than sacrifice (see Romans 12:2). If we would ask for anything from

God, let us ask Him to transform us so that what we do will be guided by Him, as we are His children. He will lead us and guide us not to conform to the things of this world, but to spiritual things, as He is Spirit.

We have so many temptations around us, but we must try by all means to resist them (see Colossians 3:5-10). We know that there will one day be a judgement, where everything we ever did will be seen. So there is no point in trying to hide anything now, as everything will appear before us on judgement day. It is that it will all not only appear, but that we will be punished for it.

HOW DO WE LIVE A CHRISTIAN LIFE?

By talking to God in prayer, we will get to know each other fully. It becomes easy for Him to understand us, and we will be understanding Him as well. That means there is an understanding of each other, and your relationship becomes strong. That is the main purpose of praying: to strengthen our relationship.

Sometimes, through the weakness of our flesh we may sin, not doing it purposely but through the weakness. We must always pray for forgiveness so that we are restored to our original state. Try to make yourself live a Christian life in such a way that you will be so used to that kind of life that you will be happy to be like that always. If you look back to the life you lived before, you will notice the difference between that life and what you are now. You will notice that you are now living a better life than you were living before. Maintain that relationship with God, and you will find satisfaction in that Christian life. You will be wishing to maintain that kind of life always.

We have got to know that Jesus died for us and also that prayer strengthens our relationship with God. We know that His ways are written in the Scriptures, by reading His Word, it tells us to love Him with all our strength and to love others as we love ourselves.

We have to be living a perfect, clean Christian life of emulating Christ Himself, who did not offend anybody or make anybody unhappy. Living the life of praising God all the time, respecting every individual because they are created in the image of God, and knowing and having faith in the salvation that Christ brings to us, we should always be praying to strengthen our relationship with God. Reading the Word of God always will make us closer to Him, knowing that we are in Christ and He is in us, and we have fellowship with other Christians.

CHAPTER 16

THE SPIRITUALITY OF THE RESURRECTION

The bond between God and humankind was sealed at the resurrection of Christ. The whole mission of Christ is to strengthen that bond, so humanity is closer now to God than before. We glorify what Jesus did to suffer all that pain for our sake. Now that we have been redeemed, we must give all the glory to Him. The souls of those who believe in Jesus's resurrection will not see a second death. Jesus did all that He did to set an example, so now we know that as we are following His footsteps, we are going in the right direction, the direction of rising in the end; that is, our souls will have a resurrection.

Jesus's resurrection gives confidence to all Christians. Despair, evil, and death with its pain all have been defeated at the resurrection of Christ. God's will was done at the resurrection, and all His plans were fulfilled. So it is for Christians to rejoice in that because it is for their good. Also, it is proof that there is life after death by the resurrection of our souls; it means victory over sin. And since we are following the footsteps of Christ, we will all rise as He did. What Jesus did was to show us that this is what is going to happen to us as well if we are following faithfully. What we are saying is not something of our making; Jesus Himself said He was the resurrection and the life. The one who believes Him will live, even though they may die; and whoever believes in Him will never die, but will live again, and will have everlasting life (see John 11:25–26).

THE SAINTS WILL RISE ON THE JUDGEMENT DAY

Christians believe that on the day of judgement, all the saints will be raised from the dead. The apostle Paul wants us to understand that it is through faith that we will be saved. It is preached that we are trying to implant this message into the people's minds that if we are following Jesus, we will be following all His steps. If there was no resurrection, even our preaching could be in vain. Let us strive to worship Him in Spirit and in truth because He is spirit.

First Corinthians 15:50–52 says flesh and blood cannot inherit the kingdom of God. That is why Christians are urged to strive to worship Him in spirit to be able to inherit eternal life. Although we suffer on this earth, this is temporal. There will be a time when death will not hold us anymore but to let the holy One go. The crucifixion and the resurrection are taken as a single event.

Christians believe in the spirituality of the resurrection, although it might appear like a physical body it will be a transformed body. What is normally happening here is the resurrection of the soul, not the body. If a person is spoken of as being resurrected, that means that person is divine, and the soul is worthy of the resurrection. That is the reason why the preachers are insisting that we stay pure so that there is no second death, but the resurrection of the soul.

FAITH IN JESUS CHRIST BRINGS SALVATION

The reason it is said it is by faith that we will be saved but not by our works, is because it is simple knowledge that God decided to save and made all the plans necessary before we even knew about it. So when we do works, we are appreciating what God did to give us salvation before we asked for it.

Christ liberated us from slavery to Satan, who wanted us to be in hell. Jesus ransomed us once and for all, but let us not delude ourselves because the devil is working overtime wanting to make that ransom useless. Faith and salvation go hand in hand because there is no way the Lord would say, "I do not know you," when you were faithful to Him. Jesus has demonstrated it for us so that we have no any doubts that there is resurrection because He has already done it for us to follow the example. What is required of us is to have faith in Him because He has shown us what will happen to us if we follow His example faithfully. If at all there was no resurrection, it would be difficult for us to convince those hearing our preaching that we would be leading them to eternal life, but now Jesus has done it for us, so for us it is now a walkover. Christ's death and rising from the dead has said it all. Whenever there appears to be death we must not see gloomy and doom but rather see life after death, called resurrection of the soul.

JESUS MAKES US KNOW WHAT HE KNOWS FROM HIS FATHER

Jesus is saying He knows the Father better than we do, but He goes on to say, "If you know Me, I will make you know the Father also," (see Matthew 11:27). He says, "If you love Me, you are not My servants but My friends" (see John 15:4–15). So the first thing is to love Him, and He will do the rest.

Jesus has made a chain of relationship in the form that He knows His Father better, but now He says, "Know Me better, and you will automatically know the Father." Yet without knowing Him, we cannot know the Father. We must not strive for anything but to know Jesus; then He will do the rest for us (John 14:7). He is saying as He is going to the Father, we must be happy that as we are His friends, we will also go to the Father. But when we talk of going to the Father, we become hesitant because it means going through death because we fear death so much, not knowing that that is our way of going to the Father.

Jesus is saying one and the same thing. Dying for us or carrying the heavy load for us, He is saying He is prepared to do everything for us because of His love to us or for us. He took His time to explain that He did not come to change the laws but only that they were misinterpreting them so He had come to make them clear. Jesus gave a very good example. He honoured His earthly parents like this: when He was found in the temple questioning those who claimed to know the laws, and His parents said, "We have been looking for you for three days," He did not refuse to go with them, but He went with them. So Jesus gave us something that we have to follow. For everything, in everyday life, He has put something that will guide us, everything we do, the way is lit by Him, every stage of our lives, He wants us to walk in a well-lit way.

What we are happy with is that Jesus imparts everything He has to us. When He was given authority over everything, He gave that authority to us when He commissioned us to go into the world and teach all nations as He Himself did. Now he is imparting the power of resurrection to us to also rise with Him as He has shown.

CHAPTER 17

THE SIGNIFICANCE OF CHRISTIANITY

Our Christian faith hinges on the life, death, and resurrection of Jesus. If there was no resurrection of Christ, what would we tell the people? But now we have the confidence to say that He is alive, and He is interceding between us and God. Christianity is the only religion that believes that there is God the Father, the Son, and the Holy Spirit. Christianity believes in the Trinity. Before the coming of Christ, people believed in God; after the coming of Christ and His ascension, those who had followed Him for three years, carried on telling people what they were taught by Christ.

Really, there is death and the resurrection of Christ. We have to be faithful that Christ died for us and that there is resurrection. To say God loved the world and gave His only Son does not help us if we do not believe that the Son was sent and died for us.

Christianity began with a very small group of people who had followed Jesus for three years. After Jesus's ascension, there was no command to start this movement. It was a sort of inspiration burning in their hearts, but that did not come so easily. They suffered persecution, which caused them to be scattered all over the place, yet it was a good turn in disguise.

People never believed them because they wanted someone to come from heaven directly for them to believe. If He was not born as a human being, people would not have believed Him either. Jesus said, even if a person came from heaven, they would not believe him; that is why He came in human form. That made them to carry this word of Jesus with them wherever they went, so this helped to spread the word easily. Within a short time, it became a religion to reckon with.

The speed with which it spread might show that there were some divine powers behind it. These divine powers would have emanated from the time when Jesus commissioned His disciples when He directed them to go and make disciples. The promise He gave was that, He would be with them all the time, up to the end of the age, so we may not be surprised when it grew so rapidly.

JESUS TRANSFERRED HIS POWERS TO US

The main purpose of Jesus coming to earth was to deliver us from the power of darkness, transferring us to the kingdom of God. That means we are going to inherit whatever is in the kingdom of God. Luke gives an example of how He did it. When He called His disciples together, He did not just send them into the village without giving them power (see Luke 9:1; 10:19–20). He is still doing the same today: He is not just sending us in the world without giving us power. He gives us His power, so we must not be afraid of doing His work, for He will be with us and He goes with us (Matthew 28:18–20).

When He is sending them out there, He is not sending them out there without any powers, when He says I will be with you means that His powers will be with us. With His power, He will get rid of the weaknesses in us and give us the courage to do what He wants us to do for the spread of His kingdom on earth. That is what the Lord wants to make the kingdom reach everyone or to reach every corner of the world. We can be the ambassadors of the heavenly kingdom on earth.

We are in a corrupt world, and we are all encountering the powers of darkness, so we need power to be able to overcome all those powers and be good workers in the Lord's field. The amazing things we saw Jesus doing, He did in order for us to know that we are also able to do that as long as we stay in good relationship with Him, because He has got all the powers to transfer to us in order for us to be able to do His work. In Colossians 1:13 Paul is pleading with us to be happy that we have Someone who loves us in such a way that He rescued us from the claws of the devil, that is, taking us from the powers of darkness to the light.

The devil controls those in darkness and does not want anyone to try to bring some light to them. If you are like that, they want to get rid of you first because they want those who are in darkness to be there forever. They control the kingdom of darkness. We are pleading with all those who would like to see the light but are being prevented by the devil to also ask Jesus to have mercy on them so that they see the light. Jesus came in order for them to see the light.

For the light to be meaningful to us we must be a changed creation. If our hearts are with the love of Christ, we will be able to show the world that we are in Christ, and that we are able to avert the power of darkness. When Jesus sent out His disciples, He made sure they were filled with the Holy Spirit (Luke 9:1).

Jesus promised that He would be with us. It appears we are doubting Him, because as He sends us out, we do not trust the assurance we were given that He would be with us. Let us trust His words, which say He would be with us. Jesus is assuring us not to fear anything because His promise was not for that time only. Difficult situations will always be with us, but He promises that they will do us no harm. Jesus is there to support us in whatever way. Ask the Lord to take away our fears so we will be able to carry on with the task that He gave to us.

Christianity is a belief that Christ was born as human, he went through a normal life as a human being, and was condemned to death, they said, for blasphemy. They claimed that all the people were following Him, that He was misleading the people. But contrary to that, Jesus was following all the laws of the state. When He was convicted, He was sentenced to death by crucifixion. When He was nailed to the cross, he died, and on the third day He rose from the dead, and now He is alive and is interceding for us between us and God.

After His ascension, a small group of His followers started a movement, because Jesus had promised them that, when He was going back to heaven, He would not leave them comfortless, but would come to them in the form of the Holy Spirit. So after Jesus ascended into heaven, His disciples spread the gospel, and started a movement called Christianity. This movement grew rapidly, spread all over the world, and became one of the most successful missions of spiritual acts throughout the world's history.

JUDAISM AND CHRISTIANITY

Judaism believes that there is one God, but they do not believe in Jesus. They believe that Jesus is one of the prophets. Christians believe in Jesus as the Son of God; they believe in the Trinity. They believe that they are guided by the three of them—God the Father, Jesus the Son, and the Holy Spirit. The Christians do not want to separate them. Judaism believes in the oneness of God, and they want to adhere strictly to the Bible's standards of social justice and hold to Yahweh as the God of Abraham. They say if He is the one who was there, and He declared that He was one and ask where we get the other two.

Jesus was born to the Jewish people, who regarded themselves as the chosen people. This kind of belief still exists and has affected the relationship that was supposed to be there between Judaism and Christianity. Yet after the ascension of Christ, many apostles were sent to go and preach to the Gentiles, and they were also filled with the Holy Spirit. This is the time when the Jews were under the rule of the Roman Empire.

Jesus's teaching was of love, and He practised love and forgiveness of sins. This is what Christians emulated and implemented throughout the world. This had an influence on the Roman Empire and throughout the entire world. Christianity was started during the Roman Empire, it spread all over the world, and became a world religion. This did not go over well with the Jews, who are still holding the belief that they are the chosen people. Christianity has become the well-known religion of the modern world. Cultures and civilisations began to view it as something to follow, and it completely changed cultures, and the world became civilised.

The values of Christianity are, love God with all your mind and all your effort, and love your neighbour as you love yourself. These values have to be upheld by Christians, so that this religion will not be diluted. This Christian religion is a strong source of social life; it gives the people the meaning of life so people may lead a healthier lifestyle.

FORCES OF DARKNESS

These forces are spiritual. They do not want to see something good but to see the negative; not having anything good, they want to see the coming together of bad things. We have mentioned above that they are causes of bad things; that is why we are always fighting these forces with spiritual armoury for the truth to always prevail. The truth is always good because there is nowhere it will be proved wrong; with the truth you will always have peace of mind.

God did not abolish darkness at creation; He only separated darkness from light. So according to Ephesians 6:12, darkness keeps on coming to interfere with our relationship with God. When we profess to be Christians, we are the number-one targets of the devil. The powers of darkness do not want to see Christianity flourish; they will not rest until they see its demise.

Let us, as Christians, know that there are two forces at war. Let us be courageous and strong. Now we are fighting against these forces not with physical weapons but with the spiritual armoury to fight these forces. There is a whole lot of spiritual wickedness, so these two are always going their parallel ways. Just as light is always associated with goodness and all the good knowledge and wisdom of God, the powers of darkness are always contradictory and are going along with evil and sin and all sorts of deprivation and despair. These forces of darkness are always opposed to the forces of light, but the light will always prevail.

The way these two fight is that once there is a presence of darkness, there is absence of light. We have a very good example of how they operate: if you walk in darkness, you can trip and fall, whereas if there is light, you can always see where you are going. We always pray to God for Him not to let us walk in darkness because we know that we can trip and fall. We always pray that we are visited with the spiritual truth, which carries with it the light.

The forces of darkness are always fighting the light, they want all things to go the way we do not like these forces do not want to see the truth because it is a weapon against them. Those forces of darkness are harmful to our Christian well-being. They are a disease in our bodies; they eat into our flesh until it is exhausted. They are eating into our Christian life.

For us to survive, we have asked for His presence in all what we do, because He will give us the strength to be able to overcome all those forces which want to sway us away from the truth and from the light (Ephesians 6:12). Make God the ruler of your life; if He is, that means the powers of darkness will not come near you because they do not want to see the light that shines near God. Evil forces and dark forces are all against the light; they are working to put it off, but the force of the light is so strong that it cannot be put off by those forces of darkness. They are working day and night trying to put off the light; that is why we are saying that we must stay on the alert and be talking to our Lord, who hears and answers in time.

There are many forces that are trying to pull Christianity down. Even though those forces are strong, we have Jesus on our side, who promised to send the Holy Spirit, and He did. The Holy Spirit will fight those forces for us. If we are following Him, He will make us live a Christian life, which is clean and well guided, to be able to resist being misled by those forces. We are reminded that God will always be on the throne and will be on our side. Without being shaken by those forces, we are relieved to know that the light will always shine in darkness.

Statistics show that besides all this, and despite all these forces, Christianity is still growing steadily. Christians must show the world that it must keep its morality. Christian morality must be upheld at all times. Our God is very much delighted in that and will call us His children. Christianity led the abolition of slavery in England and America and also led in the building of schools and hospitals as the pillars of civilisation.

THE MORALITY OF CHRISTIANS

Mostly in Christianity they encourage the people to look after themselves, which helps them stay perfect.

They derive their ideas from Jesus, who taught us to be upright always. To those who stay upright and keep His commandments, He promised salvation, which is what all Christians are praying for: to get salvation at the end. Christians want to keep their standards, as the Ten Commandments were given not to make life difficult but to have a good relationship with God.

Christianity is trying to preserve good standards—fair and just treatment of others. How we treat others should be based on how we would feel in response to such treatment. If you would feel good, then keep it up; if not, then why should you do it? God made the laws for us because He wants us to be as perfect as He is. If we are as perfect as He is, that means there will always be light around that darkness. The darkness does not want to come near the light because it does not require light.

To live a just and clean life is to uphold the moral standards of Christianity. The Ten Commandments were there to preserve the ethics of Christianity. If we try to live moral lives, we please the Lord because He wants us to be pure in His eyes. God loves us if we keep the morality of Christianity.

The ideas of Christianity are derived from those of God because God made them with some divinity in them, because He himself is divine. The principles that guide Christian morality are valuable. Christians always encourage each other to practice good deeds, which help Christians to be perfect in the eyes of God, who wants us to be good. These deeds always go hand in hand with being truthful, which frees us emotionally to be always upright. Keeping these ethics will always help us to be true Christians, who are always upright, so as to be the true children of God.

As devout Christians we have to follow certain rules, and they are not like earthly laws. They are meant to make us have a relationship with God. Following these rules will make us pure so we can qualify to stay near the Lord because He is holy.

CHAPTER 18

CHRISTIANITY AND A HUMAN MINDSET

Humans are created and made in the image of God (Genesis 1:27; Acts 17:25–28). The biggest challenge that was given to humanity was to make choices. We are given the freedom to make these choices. Sometimes we tend to abuse this freedom of choice. A person can make wrong choices, Let us pray so that we are helped to make the right choices.

We have got a very good example. A person was given the choice between eating and not eating fruit from a tree in the middle of the field, but this one chose to eat. We are given a choice between going for a short period to talk to our Creator, but instead we choose to be doing worldly things and finding some excuse for doing that. Please, God, help us.

If we fail to go to church when we are supposed to, we will try to give some very convincing reasons. What we can do to help us to move forward in the right direction is to try by all means to be true to ourselves. That means not being worried much about what people say, because we are being true to ourselves. If you are being true to yourself means you will be true to the Lord and you will be true to others.

Being true to yourself is only the starting point, because everything will come to hinge on that basis. It is always difficult to make the right choice, but it is prudent to always ask for guidance because on our own we can always make the wrong decision. But sometimes when we make the wrong decision, we do not want to admit it. We want to say, "I was right, I did it because of ..." and try to give reasons we think are valid when they are not.

We have to bear in mind that sometimes if we make a wrong choice, it may affect generations to come. Remember, the choice that was made in the garden of Eden has affected this generation. What effect are you leaving for a generation to come? If we admit the wrong choices we would have made, it may help to heal and stop in time whatever would be wanting to affect negatively the coming generation, who will not be at fault at all.

GENEROUS PROVIDENCE FROM OUR FATHER IN HEAVEN

We know that God provides us with everything that we need before we ask Him, but our praying to Him is to show appreciation and to keep our relationship with Him vital. We learnt this from Jesus, who, although He was born of the spirit and fully divine, would not stop praying. He always kept the connection by praying. This means we have to keep connected above as well, as we are emulating what our Saviour did to show us the way.

We must not lose focus on what God did for us and what He is still doing for us this day. To show appreciation, we have to tell others that God is the provider, for He provides us with all our needs and guarding us against any enemies that might want to cause harm to our bodies both day and night. This must be appreciated; in response we must revere Him and give all the glory to Him. He is worthy to be praised.

When we look at His generosity, we pray that God would give us a heart like His, that gives the rain to everyone, even to those who do not care about Him.

We are thankful for the things we have through generous providence, so let us focus on things that are good for our lives. We should be grateful and feel ready to show appreciation for the kindness He has shown to us, and return that kindness by giving glory to Him, because He worthy of that glory. A certain mental state is brought on when we realise that the higher powers provide us with the Holy Spirit. That Holy Spirit makes changes, variously associated with thoughts and feelings; we respond in thanks, and a degree of pleasure to realise that the higher powers provide us with the Holy Spirit to always guide us and to intercede or intervene on our behalf; that is, someone will be between us and God. We feel lifted in spirit for the good things that happen in our lives and have a warm feeling for those who make our lives better and those who have helped us.

God gave us emotions to prompt us to do something. Emotions are an important part of religious life for many people. Religious people have a higher level of always being truthful; what they do will not need evidence. They are able to share the feelings of others, saying, if it were me, how would I feel? They always want to do things (prosocial) that can benefit others or are in someone else's interest as well or to benefit society as a whole.

Another effect might be predicted but might not yet be actual. After a religious practice, sometimes you feel a sense of passion—a great desire for something, to give goodness and grace to others to show biblical gratitude. Our human emotions are meant to prompt us to action, including loving God with all our heart and strength, including loving our neighbours as ourselves (Matthew 22:37-39). Giving goodness and grace to others must start with the love of God, as the giver has first received from God. Extend the joy of receiving from others or from God. When you receive something from others, strive to do the same to others. As God gave His life for our sake, we must be able to give generously to others.

OUR WRONGDOINGS WILL KEEP OUR MINDS ENSLAVED

Feeling remorseful after realising your wrongdoings in Christianity is the feeling of guilt and the need for repentance for sins you have committed. Once we realise that we have sinned against God, we must seek to be cleansed by punishing ourselves as we confess. He washes our sins away in response to the sincere feeling of sorrow and regret and a feeling of remorse. We feel sorrowful for the detestation of sin with a true purpose of amendment (penitence), arising from the love of God. We also feel some inferior motives and fear of divine punishment.

"Praise be to God and Father of our Lord Jesus Christ, the Father of compassion and the God of all comfort, who comforts us all in our troubles, so that we can comfort those in any trouble with the comfort we ourselves receive from God" (2 Corinthians 1:3–4). In the New Testament Jesus is often moved to mercy through compassion. Jesus' compassion prompts Him.

To have joy in Christ, we always hope in anticipation that our God will do something good. He has already done good to us through His Son, Jesus Christ, and He will continue to do good in more ways than we can count. Let us all develop the habit of anticipating God's goodness in our lives; that is where we can find joy of life.

Jesus's compassion prompts him to mercifully love, heal, and rescue. Compassion alludes to kindness and sympathy, but there is something deeper and something more profound. Jesus's very presence in the world is the ultimate act of compassion.

The following have been associated with religion: conflict with science, curtailing freedoms, delusions, having exclusive claims to truth, fear of punishment, feeling guilty, immutability, and instilling fear in people.

Christians believe in God the Father, Jesus Christ, and the Holy Spirit; they are the Trinity. Christians believe that Christ really died, rose from the dead, and had a clear ascension into heaven. They believe in the holiness of the church and the communion of the saints and in the second coming of Christ and His final judgement.

God gave us emotion to prompt us to do something. Jesus taught that all the commandments hang on these two: loving God with all your heart and strength and loving your neighbour as yourself. It has to be known that emotions help us live in healthy relationships and stay connected to God and others.

CHAPTER 19

VIEWS OF OTHER RELIGIONS ON RESURRECTION

Although the ideologies of the Sadducees and the Pharisees seemed to be the same, they differed on the resurrection of the dead. The Sadducees did not believe in the resurrection, but the Pharisees did. The Hindus likened Christ with Lord Krishna and Lord Chaitanya. For the story of the resurrection, read Matthew 28:1–20.

Sometimes in life we have to have zeal, love, and perseverance, as shown by Mary Magdalene (who had seven demons cast out by Jesus). She woke up earlier than the others to go to the tomb. When they found that the tomb was empty, others returned home, but she persisted and persevered until she was rewarded by seeing the risen Lord. Mary had the greatest honour of being the first to see the risen Lord and talk to Him, and the first to spread the word of His resurrection. She had more information than most of the disciples had, because they had a conversation with the risen Christ when she was told not to touch Him then because He had not ascended. He told her that she should go and tell His disciples that He would meet them in Galilee (see Luke 24:1–12; John 20:1–18).

If we have a deep love of the Lord Jesus such as Mary showed, we will also be rewarded. The Bible even tells us to love our God with all our hearts and with all our strength. We are to keep that commandment at the deepest of our hearts so that our relationship with God will be strong and good (see Mark 16:1–20).

These women went to the tomb early on Sunday because of some hurdles in their way. They wanted to follow their culture of anointing the dead body before burial. They had the love for Jesus, but His death was of such a violent nature that they could not do it because Jesus was on the cross. We even hear that the man who asked to bury the body of Jesus was bold enough to ask for that permission. When the permission was granted, it was too late for anything like anointing the body because the hour had grown close to the start of the Sabbath.

Another hurdle faced by these women was that they could not buy the ointment on the sabbath day. So, early on Sunday, when they had overcome that first obstacle, they managed to buy the ointment, but because of the love of Jesus they forgot what problem lay ahead of them. How did they expect to pass through the soldiers who were guarding the tomb, for they knew that it was heavily guarded. As if that were not enough, the tomb was sealed, and it had taken very strong men to roll the stone to close the tomb. How did they expect to succeed?

My friends, let us not sit with folded hands when we are faced with the same scenario because Christianity is being attacked from all angles, one hurdle after another. The world is not stable. Wars are occurring all the time. Look at how diseases are attacking the world. Churches are being turned into pubs, while some are being turned into gymnasiums. Christianity is being attacked from all angles.

These women went out without any clue as to how they were going to accomplish their mission. They played their part and left what they could not do to

God, who did the rest. My fellow Christians, let us play our part and leave the rest to God, who knows better than us. That is why the author is saying, Christians, let us rise and start walking to the tomb with a desire to accomplish our mission. We know that the task we are faced with is a mammoth task, but should we sit with folded hands? Had the women stayed at home, they would not have accomplished what they did. They put forth some effort for something to happen.

Sometimes we are faced with disbelief such that our minds are narrowed so that we demean God and look for Him among the dead. The women who went to the tomb on Sunday morning showed a great love for Jesus. We should always strive to have such love for Jesus as well, because He also loved us by dying on the cross for us. We have to think of the love that He has for us and start to have such love for Him as well. Let us change our relationship with Him and start to have the love similar to His love to us. If we do that, we build a strong relationship with Him, a relationship that will last for ever.

We should take the resurrection of Christ seriously. It means salvation for us, because by His resurrection, He crushed the head of the serpent once and for ever.

So our Christianity is built on the foundation of the resurrection of Christ. We were bought by His precious blood; He was wounded for our salvation.

Our God is alive. When we talk to Him, let us talk to Him the way we talk to any person alive. Let us remember to confess whatever ways we have sinned against Him. If we do that, He will be happy to talk to us, knowing that He is talking to people who know Him and revere Him.

The Scriptures, which tell us about Him, are inspired. We should not read them as we read any history books. Let us read them with the divineness they deserve, and when going to church, let us remember that we are not going to a memorial club but going to talk to the holy One who looks after our lives. Let us pray that God reigns in our hearts, and let us acknowledge that all power is in His hands, and let us know that everything we see is His. Sometimes we are so preoccupied with earthly things that we may miss the target.

We should always ask the Holy Spirit to guide us so that we are not swayed with some happenings of the world and fail to recognise Jesus, who is among us in whatever we do or whoever we might be with. The resurrection must remind us to keep watch because we do not know who we are talking to at any given time. The Lord might choose to visit you through a person you know or a person you do not know, because you cannot choose for Him the form He might take in coming to you. This is very important advice to remember.

The people of those days had prophecies, but because they were oppressed politically, they missed the point because they wanted politics to solve their problems, which did not happen. From the look of things, the world has not changed much. We might miss the point as well despite the fact that the people of those days had only the Old Testament prophecy. We have both the Old Testament and the New Testament to help us, but we are still groping our way forward like sheep that have lost their direction. These disciples were with Jesus for three years but they still did not understand the prophecies; how can we claim that we are better than them?

Sometimes we have to remember that if we reflect, we may see where we have wronged the Lord or sinned against the Lord. That may be holding us back without confessing, as Peter did. At the death of Christ on the cross, he remembered that he had disowned Jesus.

Maybe things like that may have happened to us in our lives and are holding us back. Let us confess and cry unto the Lord so that He might reinstate us as He did Peter. "Lord, help us."

If the body of Jesus was stolen as they want us to believe, people know thieves have no time to fold the linen nicely (see John 20:1-25). They are only concerned with vandalising; they have no time for neatness. Our Lord handled the resurrection in such a way that no one will ever doubt it. Even though there in so much evidence, the powers of darkness are still trying to make it seem that the rising of Jesus from the dead was just a delusion. The fact is that now Jesus after the resurrection can go to heaven and come back, and now He can enter a house even if the doors are locked. But on ascension, He wanted to do it in such a way that it has proof for everyone; so many people witnessed it that there can be no more doubting that He is alive today.

Christianity derives its name from a living person. Sometimes our deeds are different from God's deeds. Jesus had all the powers, so that He could have left the tomb without the need for rolling away the stone. According to our minds we would have done that, but then, no one was going to believe the story of the resurrection. It is easy now to convince anybody of the story of the resurrection because the tomb is empty right now; no one can dispute that.

If we seek His guidance in life, He will always guide us in the right direction. If our wisdom is guided by Him, it will be one that can be fair to everyone. The graveclothes could be seen by anyone as a witness of His resurrection. What people want is to make up stories that go against the truth, but even still, the truth will prevail.

Look at what happened here: they made up stories to say that the disciples came and stole Him while the guards were asleep, but even today we know that it is false. Jesus really rose from the dead and is now alive and is in intercessions between God and us. This is not an isolated story; such things are still happening to us. We still faced with some situations which try to cast doubt on things that may be true.

With such truths, we have now to pray for the resurrection of our souls. We now know it is possible because it has been proved to us beyond any doubt that He is alive. Jesus allocated His assignment and Mary's assignment very well. He asked Mary not to touch Him; His assignment was to ascend then, to the Father, in order for the process of the Holy Spirit to start. He said Mary's assignment was to be the first preacher of the resurrection. She had to go and tell His disciples that the Lord has risen and that He had gone to His Father and their Father, and He would meet them in Galilee.

The biggest challenge we are faced with is that we do not recognize yet that Jesus has arisen. What the Lord does is to wait for you to recognise Him; then He can start the conversation with you. What are we waiting for? Let us recognise Him, and let the conversation start. Then He gives us assignments. Sometimes we are so occupied with earthly things that we fail to recognise the risen Christ standing next to us. Let us have love for Him, and everything will be flowing smoothly in life.

Jesus did not hide anything, He made it clear that His Father was our Father. The power that was given to Him in heaven and on earth He transferred to us. So what more do we want? At this point it is not exaggerating to tell the reader that we have all the power; let us make the work of the Lord go all-over the world, for He commanded us to take His gospel everywhere so that no one goes without knowing the word of the good news.

We are not misleading the reader here by saying that

we have power. This power goes hand in hand with the Holy Spirit. Please let us ask for the Holy Spirit to always guide us; let us not go without the holy One. He is our guide. Moses refused to go alone. Jesus, when giving the Great Commission, even said we would not go alone, but "I will be with you" (see Matthew 28:20).

So why should you go alone? Let us not do this job using our strength or our own wisdom, which is not from God. Let us be comforted with these words that we are not alone. In whatever we do, wherever we are with Him, let us always remember these words. Whenever we start to feel lonesome or the task seems hard for us, let us take time to talk to the Holy Spirit, who is with us all the time, throughout our lives.

Some denominations believe that Christ will rule for a thousand years before the devil is finally destroyed. They do not believe in some changes that have come to Christianity, wanting to keep the original. Some want to identify theirs as the uniquely Christian denomination. They do not believe that God can be three in one— and their beliefs distinguish them from mainstream Christianity.

Most churches agree on the resurrection of Jesus, they believe that He really died and rose from the dead on the third day. They all agree that His death and His resurrection was God's plan to save humankind from our imprisonment by Satan.

Mormons believe that Jesus is the Christ, the eternal God manifesting Himself to all nations.

There are many similarities between Hinduism and Christianity, including the use of incense, sacred bread (*prasadam*), the different altars around churches, trying to know the Bible fully, praying very often, and knowing the liturgy and some set of prayers set aside, in the expectation of making us more holy, and the Christian Trinity.

Some churches tend to define the church as the bishops, and Protestants speak of the priesthood of all believers. For authority, some of them believe that the pope cannot make errors or teach error when he speaks. Protestants do not believe in that kind of thinking; they say the pope is human and can also make mistakes, but the believe in the inspiration of the Bible because they say the writing of the Bible was inspired by God. Many conservatives believe in the infallibility of the Bible, a sort of paper pope.

Some denominations are large. Catholicism is the largest denomination of Christianity. All Catholics are Christians, but not all Christians are Catholics. A Christian refers to a follower of Jesus Christ, who may be Catholic, Protestant, Gnostic, Mormon, evangelical, Anglican, or Orthodox, or a follower of another branch of religion.

Easter is one of the principal holidays or feasts of Christianity. It marks the resurrection of Jesus Christ three days after His death by crucifixion. For many Christian churches, Easter is the joyful end to the Lenten season of fasting and preparing for Eastertime for examining ourselves and confessing our sins.

THE IMPORTANCE OF RESURRECTION SUNDAY

Jesus performed some miracles, but if we would agree that this one is a divine miracle because it is affecting us to this day, because Jesus who rose from the dead is still alive and is still with us (see Romans 1:4). We can put all the divine interpretation on it as we can because that is the truth about it, and this gives us hope and confidence.

We stand before God with happiness, knowing that He loves us (Romans 4:25). Whatever He did, He did it for us so that we get eternal life. When we say He loves us, we have the evidence. Now we know that as He did that for us, we are going to rise again after the end of life. Death is not going to hold us because we have someone who stands for us. Our Saviour set an example for us to follow. The end of processes in a cell or tissue may look like victory, yet it was defeated on the resurrection day.

What death should realise is that we are in Christ, and Christ in us, so how is it going to succeed? The only way death can win is to try to pull us away from Christ by the falsehoods of the devil, trying to tell us that Jesus's rising from the dead was just a delusion. The only option the devil has is to lure us from our Lord by false pretence. This we are not going to listen to.

When we received Christ, we received with Him everything He has. The power of resurrection that He has, we now also have. The Scriptures told us exactly what is ours and how we can claim our heritage. What belongs to our Lord belongs to us. We have the right to claim it, because already the Lord suffered for us to have it. The gospels that tell us that we the children of God are true, and we have to stay assured that eternity is ours because of the love that He shows to us.

Whatever Jesus did shows that He is inseparable

from His Father and we are inseparable from Him. That is how our relationship is with Him. The biggest assurance we have from Him is a promise that He will not leave us comfortless. The Holy Spirit will be with us all the days of our lives, meaning that we are never alone in whatever we do. We are living in hope all the time knowing that nothing will come and separate us from our relationship.

Already we have a very strong relationship because of the resurrection of Christ. Our rising after death is assured because of the bond we have made with Christ our Lord. Death is now hesitant to stand against Christ again because it knows it will be crushed. Whatever falsehood that was used on us in order that our relationship with Christ would be strained, let us repent and come to our Lord. He is waiting for us like a father who was waiting for his prodigal, who, when he saw his son, ran to meet him when he came back. Our father is saying, "All those bruises I suffered were for you. Come, I am waiting for you." Let us repent and go to our Father. He is waiting for us; let us go and claim our heritage.

The way to eternal life is by believing in Jesus Christ. When you are believing in Christ, you are now staying near Him. He is holy, so for us to be holy means we have to repent. Repentance means leaving our old way of doing things and starting to do things that are acceptable to the holy One. All this effort is for us to get eternal life in the end. If we reflect that we did a lot for the Lord, all that should not be done in vain. Let us keep our faith to the end; then we can be able to get eternal life.

Easter is the day when Christians celebrate the resurrection of Jesus. Resurrection Sunday is the name that some Christians call Easter because they do not want the name Easter. So it is the same thing but a different name. Christians believe that the resurrection proves that Jesus is the Christ (the Messiah) and the Son of God. Everything He said and did was true. They believe that the resurrection means that Jesus is still with us and is guiding us every day.

Mary Magdalene was a disciple of Jesus. According to the Gospel accounts, Jesus cleansed her of seven demons, and she financially aided Him in Galilee. She was one of the witnesses of the crucifixion and burial of Jesus and famously was the first person to see Him after the resurrection. The good thing with the resurrection is that when He was going, He promised that He would not leave us comfortless but would send the Holy Spirit. During His ascension, Jesus went into heaven, in the presence of His disciples. That is proof that He is alive, and it demonstrates the power of God.

THE ASCENSION OF JESUS

By the resurrection we now have the divine interpretation. We are able to give an account of the resurrection because Jesus Himself did it in such a way it will be traceable. He stayed forty days after the resurrection in order to prove to everyone that He had risen. Although Jesus did His resurrection and His ascension in such a way that it becomes clear, our faith is such that we still lack something. That is why we are asking Him to fill us with His Holy Spirit so that we may be able to understand the hidden divine things in the Scriptures that might save us. "We ask for an understanding of the hidden things about You. We know that they become easy and understandable if You reveal them to us through the Holy Spirit."

What He did on Ascension Day, we are also relieved to know that He did not just leave the disciples when He took them out to Bethany. Immediately before ascending, He blessed them. Since everything is passed down from the apostles to us, we must rejoice as the disciples did. They went back to Jerusalem filled with joy, we must be joyful to know that the Holy Spirit is on us. Jesus has all the proof that He is alive because He proved it in the eyes of the people beyond any doubt. We now have no problem witnessing to the people that our Saviour is alive because no one can dispute that.

God planned Jesus's mission on earth in such way that when it was finished, His ascension was necessary. People doubted when Jesus said He was the Son of God, so these are all proofs that He is really the Son of God. After the resurrection, He was able to enter the house when the doors were locked. He ascended during daylight when everyone was watching. Our Jesus is powerful. So all those who said He was not the Son of God should acknowledge this. When it is said, "This same Jesus, whom you have seen go into heaven, will come again in the same manner as you have seen Him go" (see Acts 1:11).

These are all signs that there will be a second coming of Jesus. We should not be taken un aware because we are being forewarned. That is why we keep on asking the Holy Spirit to guide us so that we get ready. The way Jesus was tempted in the wilderness is still happening to us today. The devil is out to tempt us day and night. Sometimes we do not realise that the devil is at work and he gets away with it, but I say let us be always vigilant. Always put on the armour of faith and stay alert always.

Before Jesus left, He told the disciples that they would be witnesses of in Jerusalem, Judea, Samaria, and to the ends of the world. The author is appealing to the reader that we have an assignment; this gospel must not stop with us but must keep on going all over the world.

God plans His things well ahead of time. When they happen, we only see them happening and think that they have just happened. For the ascension of Jesus to happen exactly forty days after the resurrection was not a coincidence but a planned event. This was so because there are some people who always doubt. Some of the doubts come from the devil who will try to say the rising of Jesus from the dead was just a delusion. So his staying forty days after the resurrection was to convince people that He was really risen. So however the devil wants to mislead the people with his lies, the head of the snake is crushed.

When the disciples went to Jerusalem, they were

very happy meaning that they were convinced of the resurrection. Christ could easily disappear after He had risen as He used to do, but He never wanted to do that because no one could have proof of His ascension. Jesus had said it time and again that if He did not go, the Holy Spirit would not come. Soon after He had gone, the Holy Spirit came.

Christianity today has set aside the fortieth day after the resurrection as the Ascension Day. When Jesus had arisen from the dead is when He told His disciples that all the power was given to Him from heaven and on earth. Christians believe that Jesus has got all the power and has imparted that power to us, but sometimes we underrate ourselves.

Before He ascended, He told His disciples not to leave Jerusalem. They obeyed and they were filled with the Holy Spirit. This power has now been handed over to us, so we must not underrate this power, to use it we have to claim it. That means that whatever you do, you must do it with the confidence that the power is on you. You must always recall that you were created in the image of God who has all the powers. The fact that Jesus rose from the dead gives us confidence that we will also rise when we die

CHAPTER 20

DID JESUS DESERVE THE CRUCIFIXION?

Jesus was crucified for our sins. Death by crucifixion was a penalty reserved for the worst criminals. He died such a death in order to ransom us and redeem us from the prison of the devil. The crucifixion is important for those who believe that God sacrificed Jesus, His only Son. No matter how much the devil might try to lead us astray, the Lord will always overcome that so that we get salvation, because Jesus's blood has the power to atone for the sins of humanity.

Some Unitarian and Quaker Christians do not believe that Jesus was the Son of God. The crucifixion is not of significance to them. There are Christians who believe that Jesus is the Son of God; these also believe in the Trinity and are called Quakers. The crucifixion means a lot to them.

The crucifixion of Jesus was the most horrific and the most painful and disgraceful type of death, yet all this was meant for our salvation. As this was meant to redeem us, we must respond by giving all the glory to Him. Jesus was arrested in Gethsemane, convicted of having uttered a threat against the temple, and condemned to death by a confused Pilate. The answer to the question as to why Jesus was crucified seems to be His threat against the temple.

Those who accused Him were giving different reasons. They were acting blindly because His dying for our sins was prearranged so that man should get salvation. Some accused Him of blasphemy; some said He was a father of demons. It seems that for Him to be sentenced to crucifixion was a result of some Pharisees overdoing things, as the death penalty by crucifixion was for very notorious criminals. They accused Him of blasphemy; was that notorious?

The killing by crucifixion was the cruellest kind of killing. When we are doing things, we should not rush into conclusions. Also, Pilate would have thought twice not to try to appear good to the Pharisees. Still, he said he saw no fault with Him, and he had all the power to release Him.

WE ARE GETTING SALVATION TODAY BECAUSE JESUS SUFFERED FOR US

Zacchaeus showed that he was very keen to see Jesus, and his effort was rewarded (see Luke 19:1–10). This teaches us that whatever we do, we have to show some desire to do it and some keenness. All the effort that Zacchaeus put into it was rewarded. In our lives, whatever we intend to do, we must show the desire and to put forth some effort, and we will be rewarded.

Not only did Jesus say He would go to Zacchaeus's house but that salvation had come to his house. What we are striving for in the end is salvation. Jesus looks within us and sees how clean our hearts are and also sees what effort we put into whatever we do. We have to learn that to get salvation depends on how you behave yourself.

In the same Gospel of Luke (see Luke 18:18–29), we read of a rich man who was asked by Jesus to go and sell all his wealth and come and follow Jesus, but he left disappointed. Here, by contrast, we see a man who, without being prompted, offered to sell His goods and give to the poor. This man was promised salvation; that is why earlier on we said Jesus does not care how much wealth you have got, but looks in your heart. Let us truly give our hearts to Jesus, and He sees exactly what we mean, let us come to Him without deceiving for He sees what is in our hearts.

Although the suffering of Jesus brought us salvation, it does not come on a plate, but we have to follow the example given by Zacchaeus, who knew that he was a sinner and repented. We must be able to reflect and see our past. Zacchaeus repented and was forgiven by Jesus, who knows very well that we are living in a corrupt world; so once we repent, He is faithful enough to forgive our sins. He is able to deliver our spirits from the evil spirits that want to lead us astray always (see Galatians 1:4).

When we accept God, we are saying, "God, use us the way that is better for us," and He will bring us salvation. Since we have been rescued from the sins of this corrupt world, we must live a life that pleases God because that was His reason for redeeming us. We must always ask ourselves where our loyalty is, whether it is in this world or in God (Colossians 1:13).

Paul wants us to gain knowledge, but this knowledge must be guided by God. The knowledge of God transfers us from slavery to freedom. Our relationship with God is always tainted by sin, which does not want to see us getting salvation. The Holy Spirit helps us thwart some of the evil spirits that want to separate us from God and deny us the salvation that was made for us.

If Jesus saved others from sin, He can also save us if we confess our sins. He does not promise us what He will not deliver; once He promises, He will do it. He accepted death on the cross in order to bring us salvation. We cannot earn salvation by our deeds, but we earn it by the grace of God, because the grace was there before our works, so it lies with us to be faithful. Jesus bore our punishment on Himself, so by His wounds we are saved.

Salvation has come; it is now up to us to receive it. Should anything come to your life you must show an effort to receive it. If you do not make an effort, you will not receive it. Jesus brought us salvation, so let us receive it. Only two things are required of us: dependence and faith. As the Saviour has stretched out His hand, we must also stretch out ours in order to receive what He has for us.

Since it was planned, we are saved through His suffering, and through His wounds we are saved (Hebrews 10:10–18). Everything that happened to Jesus was for the forgiveness of our sins; with His stripes we are saved (see Isaiah 53:5). Through all that suffering we now have salvation. We had gone astray and were fit for hell, but by shedding His blood on the cross, Jesus made a new covenant with us. There is no more killing of animals to atone for our sins.

Jesus did it all, so the sacrifice that is found in Jesus's blood is called a perfect sacrifice. The old covenant was bound by the law, but the new covenant is bound by the perfect blood of Jesus. When the curtain was torn during His time on the cross, it meant that there was no more need to have someone take our sins to God; rather, we can take them directly to God ourselves, confident of our salvation through the blood of Jesus.

THE NEW COVENANT WAS MADE ON THE CROSS

The second warning appears in Mark 9:30–32. Jesus told His disciples of His coming death and resurrection, but they could not understand Him. This shows that even if we are reading Scriptures, there could be something we might not understand that has to be clarified by the Holy Spirit.

At times even we ourselves fear these divine things too much to ask any questions, as the disciples did. It is relieving to know that to be able to ask questions is a sign of having faith. Faith is the opposite of fear, we are now warned that to fear is lack of faith. All that happened to Jesus, He knew it all beforehand, because all that happened was what He had come here for. "The Son of Man is going to be betrayed into the hands of man. They will kill Him, and after three days He will rise." But they did not understand what He meant, and they were afraid to ask Him about it (Matthew 17:22–23). We also ask to be given foresight to know our future beforehand. We must always ask Him to make clear our future destiny so that we are aware. Lord, remove all fears from us so that we can work for You without fear of the devil who instils fear in us.

Just as the disciples did not understand how the new covenant works, we may not understand unless the hidden things of heaven are revealed to us. Let us ask the Holy Spirit to help us to understand that through death we will be able to see the resurrection of our souls. That is the new covenant that Jesus came to make with us, and we have to follow in His footsteps. We do not have two ways but to follow His example.

If anything, let us ask God to give us a revelation so that we may be able to understand things that may happen to us in the remote future. Sometimes we think that God has abandoned us, yet He may have something in store for us that we may be failing to grasp today. Although Jesus had said before that He had brought the new covenant, it was not fully established until His death and His resurrection, When He said to His disciples that He would die and rise again, they did not understand why He should die and rise again. That is why we say, Please give us a revelation so that we are able to understand the heavenly things.

The key points of the crucifixion and resurrection: The resurrection showed that Jesus was the Son of God. The resurrection provides hope of a future resurrection, and eternal life is well grounded. The crucifixion is more important as this is when sin was overcome.

For Christians, the death of Jesus was part of a divine plan to serve humanity. The death and resurrection of one man is at the very heart of Christian faith. For every Christian it is through Jesus's death that their broken relationship with God is restored. This is known as the atonement. Jesus died on the cross as a final atonement for all sins. His sacrifice on the cross is the fulfilment of salvation for all people. All we need is genuine faith in Jesus as Son of God and Saviour, and we are eternally saved.

According to Mark's gospel, He endured the torment of crucifixion from the third hour (between approximately nine o'clock and noon), until His death at the ninth hour, corresponding to about three p.m. The soldiers affixed a sign above His head stating, "Jesus of Nazareth, King of the Jews," according to the Gospel of John.

It is going to be difficult to try to justify why Jesus could die of crucifixion which was a punishment for the most notorious criminals, yet clearly Jesus did the good works that they could see for themselves. He fed the five thousand and again the four thousand. This was all witnessed by them. He had calmed a storm and brought back the dead to their loved ones.

CHAPTER 21

THE WILL OF GOD WAS DONE AT THE CRUCIFIXION OF JESUS

God wanted to stop the blood sacrifices of animals for sins once and for all, and He also knew at the same time that the blood of Jesus would cover them once and for all. So for Jesus to be nailed on the cross was not a coincidence but was pre-planned as God's will; so when it happened that way, the will of God was done. God did that for a purpose, knowing that when it happened, it would advance His kingdom. So all that happened to Jesus on the cross made glory for Him now and for evermore.

During Old Testament times, people used the blood of animals to cleanse their sins. God had a plan to send

His Son into the world to die by crucifixion for the sins of the world. So when Jesus was nailed on the cross, the plan of salvation was carried out; that is how much God loves the world. The plan included all that Jesus had to suffer. People put a crown of thorns on His head and whipped Him with a very painful scourge which caused blood to flow and exhausted Him.

He was made to carry His own cross to Calvary where they forced nails through His hands and feet, with people mocking and spitting at Him. All this happened because it was a plan of salvation, well planned before it happened. That is why we ask God to give us a revelation so that we are able to know that all these things happened this way because of God's love for us.

As they did all this to Him, persecuting Him to this level, little did they know that He would rise again. This was done as a sign of salvation to us, but that does not mean the salivation is automatic. Jesus makes it clear that it is not all who will make it, but those who do the will of God. Let us not remain in a comfort zone at hearing the word *salvation*; we have to do the will of God to qualify for this salvation, which seems to have already come.

The plea of the author to the reader is this: let us do the will of God in order to qualify for this salvation, which was brought by the suffering of Christ. Jesus did this in order for the kingdom of heaven to come to this earth, but we must do all we can to qualify to be recipients of this salvation. Let us start practising holiness, as it is one of the requirements of this salvation. When Jesus says except those who do the will of God, it is crucial because even Jesus Himself knew a time when He said, "Let Your will be done."

Jesus sacrificed His life for our salvation and also shows that we have been redeemed from the chains of the devil, who wanted to subject us to torment forever. Let us have faith in the crucifixion of Jesus because it means a lot to us. Jesus's suffering and dying on the cross was a redemption to us because we were ransomed and redeemed by His blood. This means we are no more bound by the law but by faith. We have to be faithful to Him, and His grace is sufficient.

WHAT IS SIN?

Obeying God is part of resisting sin. We mostly ask not to be led into temptations. If temptations are away from us, it means we may be able to avoid sinning. Obeying means you will be staying near holy places; sin does not want to stay near holiness. God sent His Son into the world to suffer and die on the cross. When that happened, His plan of salvation was done. God is working to restore the radiance (light or heat reflected by something) of His own glory through us.

Although Jesus was betrayed by His own disciple (Matthew 26:49), the disciples were called the inner circle of Jesus. It teaches us not to hate but to always be on the alert about those close to you. They know you well, know where you are all the time, and know your weakness. Sometimes our enemies are people who know us better, not strangers who know nothing about us.

If we ask why Jesus was not resisting, we see that the plan of salvation could not be accomplished. We have to be very careful when we profess to be the disciples of Jesus. Our deeds might be like those of Judas: we might be betraying Him with our deeds.

Sometimes we find that problems are so big that we tend to forget and start thinking that the Lord has forsaken us. We forget that to overcome them, we have to ask for the guidance of the Holy Spirit. When Jesus foresaw the pain that was ahead of Him, He asked for help (Luke 22:42). We should be able to emulate Him and say, "Your will be done, not my will," but sometimes we forget that part of prayer, of submitting ourselves and letting His will be done.

When we are praying, we are following in Jesus's footsteps. We have to give God His place, knowing that He is on the throne. Our lives were predetermined; in return, we have to put ourselves in His hands and say, "Your will be done, not my will." Jesus is teaching us here to submit ourselves to the will of God, who loves us.

It is God's will to save humanity from the chains of the devil, who wants to separate us from our relationship with God. The will of God was to save us from the devil by making His Son die on the cross so that His blood would save us from our sins. When Jesus was being sacrificed on the cross, the will of God was done. That is why Jesus said, "It is finished," meaning that things had gone according to plan. Now people are able to go to God through Jesus Christ without shedding the blood of animals; the blood of Jesus is sufficient to cleanse our sins. We are following in the footsteps of Jesus, who taught us a very valuable lesson: when He had seen a tough time ahead of Him, Jesus wished it would not happen, but He knew that He would not do things His own way. That was why He said, "Let your will be done." This has to be our guidance whenever life gets tough. We can learn to say, "Your will be done." That means we are giving God His place. We are His vessels; He must mould us according to His will. That means we have surrendered ourselves to Him. If we live according to what God wants (John 5:19), that means we will have unity with God. If there is good will on our part, the Holy Spirit will help us to accomplish our goal. But it should never be that we ask the Lord to do His will and we do the opposite; we have to comply and do as He tells us to do.

During the time of the Old Testament, people used the blood of animals to cleanse their sins. God had a plan to send His Son into the world to die by being crucified on the cross. When He was nailed on the cross, the will of God was done; that is the ultimate pattern of loving the world.

When Jesus saw the pain that was ahead of Him, He had to say, "If it is possible, You could let this cup pass; nevertheless, not My will, but Your will be done" (see Luke 22:42). God sent us here on a mission, so sometimes we meet with some temptations that induce us to forget to give God His place and let His will be done. When we are in prayer, we are following in Jesus's footsteps. We have to give God His place, knowing that He is on the throne. Some of our lives were predetermined; we have to put ourselves in His hands. When Jesus said, "Let your will be done, not my will," He was teaching us to submit ourselves to the will of God, who loves us. Sometimes we are faced with situations which are very difficult to determine on our own, using our flesh and blood, but we need to leave everything with Him, for He knows what is good for us.

LET US ASK GOD TO GIVE US A REVELATION

Jesus was about to undergo the most difficult struggle of His life, the crucifixion. Already seeing what was ahead of Him, Jesus had to plead with God to make that cup pass, but not as He wished but the will of God be done. The Bible says Jesus was in agony. We can see from the intense conflict in Jesus's prayer that He was demonstrating how we have to submit ourselves to the will of God.

The reason why we pray that God should give us a revelation is because sometimes we are faced with situations in which we sometimes give up; yet in future they may have fulfilled the will of God if we had persevered. That is why we are asking for a revelation so that God is sending us on a mission that we must accomplish. We were given a good example by Jesus, who prayed His way through a time so hard that as he prayed, His sweat contained great droplets of blood (Luke 22:44). He asked His Father to remove the cup of suffering, but then He surrendered: "Not My will but Your will be done."

When we pray, "Your will be done on earth as it is in heaven," we are praying that something will happen in earth that has never happened before. We are praying that God will bring about His heavenly purpose on earth. We are praying that God will use us to do His will on earth.

We all want to walk in the Spirit. When you walk in the Spirit, it means you have God's revelation, because walking in the Spirit, you are walking under guidance. Sometimes God gives us a revelation, but we do not recognise that it is a revelation, and we ignore it and lose out. Sometimes when we say, "God, give us a revelation," we are saying, "God, help us to recognise when the revelation comes to us." Most of the time, the revelation is very quiet, so quiet that you may not recognise it is a revelation. Let us try to answer those whispering voices, which sometimes seem very remote.

What we are sometimes faced with at such times is that even though the Holy Spirit is supposed to guide us and tell us, we fail to acknowledge Him. Wherever we go, we are with the Holy Spirit, who will guide us and tell us what to do always, what to accept and what not to accept. Let us bear in mind that revelation is those things that are communicated to our minds. Since we are thinking all the time, we will say it is our normal thinking. Like that it becomes difficult to separate them as general, special, and divine; they may appear alike and work one for the other, but there is a very thin dividing line.

When these revelations come to us, they may give us wisdom or some knowledge of a situation or enable us to tell good or bad. Our response should be always to obey those words when they come to us. That is, we must always have faith that the Holy Spirit is with us and follow what it tells us to do. Always trust that the Holy Spirit will guide you well.

CHAPTER 22

WHAT SHOULD WE DO TO BE ACCEPTED AS THE CHILDREN OF GOD?

Receive Jesus with all your faith. Those who have received Him and who have faith in Him have been made the children of God (1 John 3:10). Receiving Christ should means more than a statement by word of mouth; it must be seen in our deeds.

The best thing for us to do is to let the Holy Spirit live in us because if He is living in us, it means we will not be doing our own things but the things that the Holy Spirit tells us. He will guide us away from the things that might defile our bodies, our flesh, or our spirit. This Holy Spirit will give us new hearts if we are like that; it will mean He has helped us to be like Christ, which will make us qualified to be called the children of God (Titus 3:5).

The kingdom of God is governed by love. For us to qualify, we have to love God and love one another as He loved us. If we love Him, His grace is on us, for we are saved by His grace alone and not our deeds, only through His grace and mercy (Ephesians 2:8–9). We know very well how much He loved us, so, in return we must give all the glory to Him; that will seal our relationship with Him. If anything, we have to reflect and know that we are representing God here on earth. Whatever our behaviour, we must represent the Creator to all creation because that is what He meant by saying "Let us make man in our own image" (Genesis 1:27), and the fact that we were given dominion over everything must make us humble ourselves to be respected.

Believers must be happy that we were adopted through Jesus Christ to be the sons and daughters of God (Ephesians 1:5). It appears we are fearful to claim that we are sons and daughters of God. Let us claim our rights, which were bestowed upon us by the death of Jesus on the cross. If we are not afraid to claim our standing as children of God, we are acknowledging the death of Christ on the cross as that suffering for us (Romans 8:15). Once we are called the children of God, that means we are going to inherit all that is God's; there is nothing to prevent us from claiming that inheritance once we are called the children of God.

What we have to do is obey the Holy Spirit, who will always guide us in the path that will lead us to where we are supposed to be. The Holy Spirit guides us to identify with Jesus, who is the Son of God. He has even said, "Be in Me; I am in the Father." That is how we will be interwoven with them. Let us be good and be holy, and everything will be in place automatically.

Jesus said clearly that He is in the Father, so He and the Father are one. He went on, "And also be in Me, and I will be in you," which means if we have faith in Him and He is in us, then automatically we become the children of God (1 John 3:10). All this is pointing to us to be born of the Spirit, there is no way you can do things that do not please God if you are born of the Spirit, and if what you do pleases God, there is no way He can say you are not His child. So what is required of us is to truly love Jesus; that means we will be doing His will always if act as the children of God.

There should be no problem in identifying the children of God, for they shall be known by their deeds and by their fruits. For example, one day Nicodemus came to Jesus by night and said, "No matter what people are saying about you, it is clear by your deeds that you have come from God" (see John 3:2). For us to be like that, we have to surrender ourselves to His will. This comes back to us so that we will be loving Him with all our minds, strength, and energy, which means we will be loving Him wholeheartedly. Then it goes on to say that if we love God like that, we will love one another because God is love, and His law says love one another as you love yourselves.

When we teach our children as they grow, we should teach them to value other children, relatives, and other people. If they practice that from childhood, they will be leading others in loving one another. That behaviour in itself shows them to be children of God. It sometimes becomes difficult to show love, but if there is no response from the other side, it is our duty to demonstrate or teach by our deeds.

Practise to love, to be respectful, and to be tolerant of others. When the actions of others tend to upset you, learn to accept them. Sometimes things get bad, but persevere and keep your goodness. Remember that you know the truth, and you are trying to help others know it. It takes time. The grace is meant to make us the highest people, not to make us slaves; it is there to exalt us and not to demean us. Our Father has all power; as the children of God, when that power is imparted on us, we should not abuse it, not looking down upon other people or other things. Respect for everything is what is important.

LET US SUBMIT TO THE AUTHORITY OF GOD

Obeying God is part of resisting sin. Submitting to the authority of God means you will be staying near holiness. Sin does not want to stay near holiness (Romans 7:25). God sent His Son into the world to suffer and die on the cross: then His plan of salvation was done. God is working to restore the beauty of His own glory through us.

It is acceptable to have some authorities here on earth, but above all those authorities there is one above them (1 Peter 2:13–25). This authority is the one we must submit to. Jesus knew that there is a higher authority, the authority of God. At one time He said,

"Give Caesar what belongs to him"; by doing that, you will live a good life. The good life of a Christian will bring many to God. We want to win to God as many souls as we can. Your words, deeds, and actions and your faith should all bring souls to Christ.

This makes reflect again because we seem to very much want to be submitting willingly to the authority of this world instead of submitting to the authority above all authorities. Yet the reason is simple: from the authorities of this world we want to get favours. What we forget is that those authorities we want to get favours from also have a higher authority and must pay their allegiance to it. That authority is good because it rules with loving kindness.

To submit to this authority is to empty yourself and say, "God, mould me the way You like and the way You think I should be, into a good vessel of Yours that You can use the way You want to, so that I can be productive to the growth of Your kingdom. Lord, You can use the Holy Spirit that is in me for the good of Your kingdom" (Luke 10:19) The relationship is built like this: we start with obedience to God, which means we very much want to do the work that advances His kingdom. Then He will increase His authority over us.

Receive Jesus with all your faith. Those who have accepted Him into their hearts, and those who have faith in Him, He has made them the children of God. The laws of God are unlike the laws of this earth which when you submit to them you appear like a slave. Yet when you submit to the authority of God, you build a good relationship with God.

ACCEPT JESUS INTO YOUR HEART

To all who receive Him and believe in His name, He will give them authority to become the children of God (see John 1:12). To receive Jesus into your heart means to be reborn, and it means He lives in you and will transform you. Then people will not see you as you were before.

First, accept His word as truth, regard Him as your Saviour, and welcome Him into your heart, and the rest will follow. Our beliefs and our faith must be the ones that will cause us to surrender ourselves to Him so He uses us and makes us become the children of God. Let us love God with all our hearts and also love our neighbours as He commands us to do. So we will become His children.

We should reject Satan every day of our lives and accept Jesus as the Saviour. What Jesus went through on the cross was for you and me, we are to accept Him in our hearts as the one who has our eternal life at heart. Obey and fulfil all Christian obligations and those of the state also.

We are obligated to win more souls to Christ as per the Great Commission. It is part of the agreement to become the children of God that we are to carry out the assignment that we were given. We were all created for a purpose, to ensure that we spread His word to reach everyone, so that everyone knows that we have a Saviour who loves us. We must be the preservers of Christianity, for we are the stewards of the Lord on earth. If we choose to obey and walk in His ways, He will pour His Spirit on us to become His children who carry His image.

If you are always in prayer, that means you are always talking to your Father, which makes you the child of the Father. To be in prayer is to be talking to God, so as to build the relationship of Father and child. Be active in all the Christian works, and obey His commandments; seek to be in communion with Him all the time, and always be truthful.

Have you ever accepted Jesus's way of living? That is, have you accepted Him into your heart? His way of living is loving. If we follow that, it means we will be living a life like His life. leading us all to eternity.

CHAPTER 23

COSMOLOGY AND THE EXISTENCE OF GOD

In the Bible, cosmology is the biblical writers' conception of the cosmos as an organised, structured entity, including its origin, order, meaning, and destiny. All Christians agree that God is responsible for all creation. Christians agree in believing that cosmology and Christianity go hand in hand, knowing that each plays its own part.

Cosmology is a branch of astronomy that involves the origin and evolution of the universe, from the Big Bang to today and on into the future. According to NASA, the definition of cosmology is the scientific study of large-scale properties of the universe as a whole. The study is still going on to know how the universe has changed and how it will look in the future. The study helps us know who we are and where we came from.

In Christianity, cosmology draws us to try and understand God, the cosmos, and the place of human beings in relationship with God. In religion, cosmology is the religious conception of the world and particular phenomena in the world. The third way is the cosmological argument; in natural theology is an argument that claims that the existence of God can be inferred from facts concerning causation, explanation, change, motion, contingency, or finitude, with respect to the universe and some totality of objects. There certainly is no shortage of arguments that purport to establish God's existence, but argument for the existence of God focuses on three of the most influential: the cosmological argument, the design argument, and the argument from the religious existence.

WHAT DOES GOD WANT US TO DO?

Sometimes we try to hide ourselves from God, but His love to us is that He looks for us each time we try to hide from Him. It is just as in the garden of Eden, when He called until Adam admitted that He was hiding. It is a matter of trying to emulate Him. It may seem that He is compelling us to love Him, yet He is the one who loved us first. We are living for a purpose; once we know that, He bestows divinity in us so that we become like Him. God desires to see us joyful and not miserable, when we think that we are taking the wrong way.

God's word can change us and give us meaning of life. Reflect and see what you did in your life before, and pray for forgiveness. Let us seek wisdom from Him through the Holy Spirit, not human wisdom, which will lead us astray. Whenever we are thinking of serving Him, let us serve Him in spirit and in truth.

CHAPTER 24

WHAT WAS JESUS'S MISSION ON EARTH?

As Jesus came, now we understand what the kingdom of heaven means, because He taught us what the kingdom is. When Jesus came, it was declared that the kingdom of God had come, which brings eternal hope to all those who believe. As soon as He came, our relationship with God changed. Because of His coming, we made a new covenant with the Lord.

His main aim is that we know and believe in God so that in the end we will be assured of eternity. This was impossible to talk of before, but now we can say it with certainty. We were prisoners of the devil, but He came to set us free. We were blinded spiritually by the devil, but He came so that we see. Jesus came for the broken-hearted; He came for the despised and the marginalised. So if you want a good relationship with Him, make sure you do not look down upon these people, because His eye is on them.

Jesus came to earth to preach the good news and to give people an understanding of the kingdom of God and the eternal hope that they had through Him. His mission was for the poor and the oppressed, to free all prisoners. The people of the world will keep on asking if you were once imprisoned, which means they keep that record, but with God everything will be blotted out and they will see a new creation.

We have to be careful when we do wrong to any of these people because Jesus did not mince His words. We know very well that He said, "God is spirit," and He said, "The Spirit of the Lord is upon Me" (Luke 4:18), which means He is very much concerned. We must always remember not to bring a curse upon ourselves, because He keeps an eye on them. When He says He has come to give sight to the blind so that they can see, surely spiritually we are blind. We must ask Him to make us see with spiritual eyes; that is when we begin to see the greatness of God and begin to humble ourselves to the things that are godly. When we do that, it means our relationship with Him will be renewed. He has said it clearly that he is making a new covenant with us; this covenant is strengthened with His blood on the cross at Calvary. Jesus came to set us free from the chains of Satan, but we are still saying let us stay in those chains. Yet Jesus declared "the year of jubilee." Let us rejoice that we have been set free.

JESUS CAME TO RECONCILE OUR BROKEN HEARTS

Jesus mended those broken relationships by showing love. Our relationship with God had been broken by the devil, who never wanted to see us having a relationship with our Father. Jesus came to reconcile us, because whatever wanted to move us far away from our Father, He brought us closer because our sins made us to hide ourselves from the Father (2 Corinthians 5:18). So it is up to us to take that outstretched hand of Jesus, which is saying, "Come to the fold; you are welcome." If we are staying away, it is because of the fear of our nakedness; we cannot look at Him face to face as we used to do before.

We have a very good example in the things we use daily. If anything is broken, it is thrown away and never to be used anymore. Jesus came to mend those things which were broken so that they are reusable. Since Jesus came, we are worthy to stand in front of God again and claim our heritage and all our rights which were stolen by the devil. We have to claim them back.

Our hearts are broken, and our spirits are broken; now it is time to stay with Jesus because He is our advocate. He is advocating for our property that was stolen by the devil. We are saying to Jesus, "Go and claim our everything." Instead of walking away from God, we should be walking towards God because we have someone representing us. Jesus came to reconcile a broken world and to put into a right relationship all of creation and bring a kingdom of righteousness, peace, and justice. Jesus came to earth to save people from their sins. He died on the cross in order to save us from our sins, through His life, death, and the resurrection. The reason to restore us to our original place is for us to have eternal life. He even said, "No one goes to the Father but through me" (see John 14:7). Saving us from our sins is the greatest joy that Jesus has brought for us.

JESUS CAME TO INTRODUCE THE HEAVENLY KINGDOM

Jesus wanted people to understand that His mission on earth was to introduce the kingdom of heaven, but people could not understand that. Instead, they were asking when the kingdom would come. He replied that the kingdom of heaven was already there.

Jesus came to teach and to discuss the heavenly kingdom. What Jesus taught was that after death comes the heavenly kingdom, and He encouraged people to work towards heaven. This is good news, revealed through the gospel and its ethics and how they affect us. Sometimes we tend to forget that the kingdom of heaven is our life application. What we do is inseparable from the heavenly life. This kingdom is a spiritual kingdom. Once we know that, we will be able to understand that we have to ask our Creator to transform us so that whatever we do should be spiritual. That will qualify us to be called the children of the Highest.

As Jesus proclaims the gospel, it is good news that He is proclaiming. If we commit that to our hearts, it will mean eternal life for us. If we turn away from our original desire to see the heavenly kingdom coming in a physical form, that means we will be transformed ourselves to receive it spiritually. God does the rest because He takes care of His kingdom, and it is for His glory that He does everything to protect it. That is His will; as we always say, "Your will be done on earth as it is in heaven."

MAN WAS GIVEN A CHOICE FROM THE VERY BEGINNING

Adam was given a choice from the very beginning that he must not eat of a tree in the middle of the garden. He was told from the very beginning, "If you eat, you will die," but he made a choice to eat and die (Genesis 2:16–17). Look at it closely; we still have a choice even to this day, and we are choosing to disobey. Jesus's mission on earth was to save us from that choice—a human decision which causes death in us. God gave Adam a choice because He had made him in God's own image, worthy of all respect. But unfortunately, Adam made a wrong choice, which resulted in us all facing a death penalty.

Then Jesus came to reverse all that, which is why we are saying we have been given a second chance. Let us not lose that chance again; let us take Jesus seriously this time. He wants to see us through to eternal life.

Although humanity made a wrong choice, we still have dominion over everything, as He gave us this dominion at creation. We are still to keep on asking the Holy Spirit to keep on guiding us to make the right choice, because we are still faced with the same decision whether to follow Him or not; that is a very important choice we are still to make. We are still to make a choice that following Him will give us eternal life. It is wrong on our part to think that we can do it on our own without Him, yet He is still the Creator and still controls our lives and our destiny.

Jesus's mission on earth was already explained when the Lord told Adam, Eve, and the serpent what would happen to each one of them. This is where Jesus' mission was pronounced. His main mission was to crush the head of the serpent (Genesis 3:14–15), which took place on the resurrection day when death was defeated.

THE MAN MADE A WRONG CHOICE

Our Christian lives are shaped by the decisions we make in our lives. That is why it is better to always make an informed decision. Always our decisions should be guided by the Holy Spirit.

The prophecy in Zechariah 9:9 was fulfilled five hundred years after it was predicted. That shows us that the Lord fulfils His promises. We must be warned that the second coming of Christ is definitely a reality. Let us keep ourselves as pure as we can, so that we do not have to run away anymore, looking for a hiding place because we are naked.

When the wise men said they were looking for the newborn king of the Jews (Matthew 2:1–2), there was already a confusion of thinking that He was going to deliver them from the rule of the Romans, yet His mission was to bring eternal life. The mission of Jesus on earth was to redeem the people through His blood, to deliver people from the bondage of Satan after crushing the head of the serpent. His blood is called perfect blood because it has the power of atonement. Through His blood we are redeemed. We are ransomed from the hands of the devil, who does not want to see us going to heaven. But through God's grace, we are now fit for heaven. The Messiah these wise men were looking for was not a political leader as the Jews were mistaken, but the promised soul redeemer. We must ask for a revelation so that we do not fall into that trap as well. Are we not falling into the same mistake as well today? Let us watch out.

THE WISE MEN WERE LOOKING FOR THE PROMISED MESSIAH

This confusion went on and on until even up to Jesus's triumphal entry into Jerusalem, when His heart bled because the whole crowd was happy for the wrong cause. They expected that their political freedom had come, when Jesus knew very well that He had not come for that. He knew that in the coming days the same people were going to cry out for Jesus to be crucified because their expectations were not met.

Let us ask to be made divine so that we do not celebrate for the wrong cause. On this, we have to ask for spiritual eyes so that we can be able to see things that are spiritual so that we do not think of the Messiah as a political leader as they did. The Scriptures are there to tell us of the coming judgement if we consult them spiritually.

The wise men found Him because they were guided by the Holy Spirit (Micah 5:2). We must be guided by the Holy Spirit to find Him. The wise men came from very far searching for the Messiah; we must also do what we can to search for the Messiah. God plans all that He does well ahead of time. With our little minds, when something unfavourable happens to us today, we may say that God has abandoned us; yet He has something good in store for us in the future. What we might meet today and think of as hardship may have been experienced as well in those old days. Let us rejoice in this one because God has clearly told Satan that his head will be crushed at the resurrection (Genesis 3:15). Although Satan is still striving to deceive Jesus's followers, his head has already been crushed. All the tactics he is trying to employ are mere pinpricks, not nearly as deadly as the crushing of the head. The author is appealing to the reader to say to rejoice in what Jesus did for our salvation. Now we have salvation through His suffering on the cross and His resurrection. Amen!

To know more about Jesus, we must read the Scriptures because all His ways are in the Bible. Nothing is hidden about Jesus. You can talk to Him through prayer, because that is the only way you communicate with Him. Remember, it is not just communicating with Him, but we must confess first. Then, as pure as we can be, we can communicate with Him. When you do good to others, you are doing the work of Jesus because that is what He wants us to do, to love one another. If we do that, we will be following His example, because He loved us.

Printed in the United States
by Baker & Taylor Publisher Services